Living Life Beyond

FIGHTING BACK

Defining Moments in the Life of an
American Hero, Tom Burnett, by

Deena Burnett

With Anthony Giombetti

Fighting Back by Deena Burnett with Anthony Giombetti
Copyright © 2006 by Deena Burnett and Anthony Giombetti
Editor and contributing writer: Elizabeth Burgard Fulgaro

ISBN: 1-59755-037-X

Published by: ADVANTAGE BOOKS™
  www.advbooks.com

Library of Congress Control Number: 2006926343

Cover by Pat Theriault and Kevin Murphy
Burnett Family Portrait by Kevin Murphy

First Printing: May 2006
06 07 08 09 10 11 12   9 8 7 6 5 4 3 2
Printed in the United States of America

Table of Contents

This book is dedicated to my husband, Tom Burnett, for the love he gave, the wisdom he shared, and the values he taught. I would rather have been married to him for a few short years than spend a lifetime with a lesser man.

Acknowledgments

My parents: Mom, Dad, and Cindy, thank you for giving me faith, love, and self-esteem.

My children: Halley, Madison, and Anna Clare, for their patience and devotion.

My in-laws: Mr. Tom, Mrs. Bev, Martha, and Mary for your support and friendship.

My friends: So many of you held my hand and made me smile when I didn't want to.

Every person who waved a flag, made a banner, held a candle, or offered a prayer. You made a difference in my life that you are unaware of.

Beth for believing in this project all along and for helping in the 9th hour to see it through.

Sharon Dymmel for being persistent in seeking a publisher.

Amy Rennert for her advice and guidance.

Kevin Murphy, artist extraordinaire. Thanks so much for your design!

Gene McCaffrey and Stann Leff for introducing me to Anthony, who enlisted the faithful help of Angela, Sandra, Tracy, and Taylor.

Deena Burnett with Anthony Giombetti

Preface

Five years ago the last words my husband spoke to me were: "We're going to do something."

Tom Burnett was a passenger on United Airlines Flight 93 on September 11, 2001. He and his fellow passengers were the first to ever fight back against terrorism. They gathered information, assessed the situation, and in the tradition of our great nation voted to change their destiny. They arose from their seats and did something. As a result, thousands of lives were saved, and our government buildings are still standing. They are American heroes.

However, they were not born heroes. Heroes are made. Their actions were the result of a lifetime of heroic acts built on the solid foundation of character, conviction, and courage.

Heroic acts are the result of doing what is right in the face of obstacles or opposition. The significance of a heroic act is not measured by its size, but by virtue that it was the right thing at the right time and it was acted upon.

You don't have to be a CEO, a teacher, a preacher, or a doctor. You don't even have to be an adult. You don't have to be on stage or have a spotlight thrust upon you. And you don't have to have a tragic story to be a hero. You just have to do what's right.

Tom used to say to me, "If you don't stand for something, you'll fall for anything." He was so right. Today our convictions often are not well thought out, so we become like weather vanes turning toward the argument of the day. Carefully and methodically thinking through the information helps establish our own convictions. Convictions then provide the guidepost for the direction in which we should go.

Character helps determine our convictions, and courage helps us fight for those convictions.

Character, Courage, and Conviction. They were demonstrated on Flight 93. To be everyday heroes, then we must demonstrate these in our daily lives through the decisions we make, the interactions we have, and by reaching out and helping those around us.

Obviously, from one perspective the heroes of Flight 93 were failures. They did not succeed in their plan to wrestle control back from the terrorists and land the plane safely. Their failure cost them their lives.

But they had done the right thing and from the ashes of the crash site came something almost greater than if they had succeeded. By their right choices and acts of heroism, and the outcry that followed their undeserved deaths, we were reminded that there is a greater good that we serve beyond ourselves.

Fighting Back is not just another 9/11 book. It's been five years. It is long past time to move on. That too, is the right thing. But we must never forget what happened to us personally and as a nation that day. There are important lessons from September 11th we need to take with us to lead better lives today. One of these lessons is that we each are compelled to pick ourselves up and "do something".

Fighting Back tells Tom's story and my story. In and of ourselves, Tom and I are nothing special. He was and I remain ordinary people. But perhaps our story will inspire you to see how each of us can have a positive effect on the world beyond ourselves simply by the choices we make.

Flight 93 reminded us that true heroism is something more than being admired for what you do well. Instead, when you become a true hero – by doing what is right in the decisions you make – your character, conviction, and courage will lead to actions that impact our world with greatness. At times, doing what is right means **Fighting Back.**

Here is our story….

Chapter One

Thomas E. Burnett, Jr.
Built on a Strong Foundation

"All actual heroes are essential men, and all men possible heroes." – Elizabeth Barrett Browning

The courageous actions taken by the heroes on Flight 93 on September 11, 2001, were neither random, nor by chance. In fact, they were predictable. The strength of character, which their actions required, had been forged in these individuals long before they each happened to take their seats on the plane that morning.

This was definitely the case for Tom. Since his birth, each time he made the right choice, in light of his experiences and circumstances, God began to build in him the strong foundation of faith, character, courage, and conviction, which would enable him – no, *compel* him – to be who he was on September 11th.

Before Tom Burnett was catapulted into the public spotlight by becoming one of a group who stormed the cockpit of a commercial airline in an attempt to take it back from hijackers and save our country from further attack, Tom was a son, a husband, a father, a brother, an executive, and a friend. To understand who Tom was before September 11, 2001, is to understand why he did what he did. Let me introduce you to Tom Burnett, the man.

Thomas Edward Burnett, Jr. was born May 29, 1963, in Bloomington, Minnesota. His father was a high school English and Literature teacher. His mother was a real estate agent.

From birth, Tom was a fighter. He was born prematurely and given last rites twice because he wasn't expected to survive. He was the second of three children. Tom had an older sister, Martha, whom he called Mart, and a younger sister, Mary.

Tom was a very quiet toddler and didn't really begin to talk until he was around 4 years old. But once he began, he spoke in complete sentences with a vocabulary beyond his young age.

The Burnett family lived in a suburb of Minneapolis, across the street from a 2,000 acre nature reserve, with trails, lakes and a lot of wildlife. Their house was within walking distance of their church and school. There were lots of kids his age in the neighborhood making for plenty of camaraderie and play time.

It was through his father that he gained his great love of books. Tom Sr. didn't like for the children to watch TV. He wanted them to read. Tom laughed at the childhood memory of hearing the garage door open and he and his sisters scurrying to turn off the television and grab a book. Savvy to his children, Tom Sr. would often come in and put his hand on the top of the TV to see if it was warm.

Summers were spent together on a lake in Northern Minnesota where his father worked at a summer camp as a reading teacher. Tom's mother would sunbathe while her son spent hours fishing on the dock. He would get up each morning and dig his own worms, then cut them in half so they lasted longer, giving him more fishing time! He was so small his mother wouldn't let him stand near the edge, so he had to fish through the cracks in the dock. True to the amazing man he became, Tom still managed to catch several large bass that way, some of which his parents had mounted.

Family was always of utmost importance to Tom. He made specific life choices in order to spend more time with them. He was also close to his sisters. When they were smaller and his parents would tell him, "No", Tom would go to older sister Mart for consolation and assistance. When he was in college, younger sister Mary frequently visited. He valued these visits and enjoyed showing her around campus and introducing her to his friends.

After spending time with his grandparents in Iowa once, he decided he wanted to be called T.J. (for Tom Jr.) because it could be confusing to have two Toms in the house. His family tried it for awhile, but the name never stuck.

Tom loved sports, especially hockey. He once showed up at hockey practice with figure skates because his parents had gotten a good deal on them. He was embarrassed but tried to play in them anyway. Because of the expense of hockey, his parents encouraged him to play football instead. His natural leadership skills fit the position of quarterback well. His ability coupled with a powerful arm enabled him to lead his high school team to the state championship his senior year. He was recruited by several universities to play football, finally choosing the Air Force Academy on a commission. He later went to St. John's University (Collegeville, MN) on a football scholarship. When a shoulder injury prevented him from playing football at SJU, Tom transferred to the University of Minnesota where he became President of a co-ed business fraternity, Alpha Kappa Psi.

Tom was always popular in school and known for his sense of humor and quick wit. He was the guy everyone wanted to be around. He had a magnetic personality and never minded being the center of attention. He made good grades with no effort.

His Faith

Tom once told me that even though believing in God required a leap of faith, (because in the end it could not be proven), there was more value in believing, than not believing. If all things were balanced in the fact that Biblical scholars could prove the validity of only some of the Bible stories and scientists could prove only some of their theories, then why not choose to live by that which offered the best, most rewarding way of life. "It makes more sense to believe in God," he said. "It leaves you more fulfilled than not believing in anything at all."

Tom's faith in God was strong, but it had only become so after being tempered by a refining fire. He was raised Catholic and faith was a focal point of family life growing up. As a toddler he would go up to the front of the church and sit on the steps leading up to the altar. There he would quietly, patiently sit and listen while the priest gave his sermon and then Tom would watch the Mass. Martha was at an age where this embarrassed her, but Tom's parents were thrilled. They thought at one point, he may become a priest.

During high school and early college, Tom went through an agnostic period where he wasn't sure what he believed. Though his parents were devout, Tom became a skeptic. He studied philosophers like Nietzsche, who at times also had struggled with his faith.

Ideally, Tom wanted proof for whatever he chose to believe. During his freshman and sophomore years at St. John's, a Catholic university in St. Joseph, Minnesota, he sought out the resident monks regularly to debate matters of faith. Through these discussions, the monks were able to walk Tom through his doubt until a new and stronger faith emerged. For the remainder of his life, Tom attributed the faith upon which he relied so much to the debates he had enjoyed with these monks. Had it not been for them, he might never have found the basis for the faith which gave him so much inner peace, direction in life, and enjoyment.

Tom liked the Catholic Church. He found the beliefs upon which it was founded to be thoughtfully compiled and well-researched. He liked the fact that their positions had been studied and agreed upon by hundreds of people, versus just one. It appealed to him that the heads of the church spent years deliberating their positions.

At his core, Tom was a free and independent thinker, but he was also fiercely loyal. He understood the importance of following leadership and submitting to the chain of command. Therefore, once he committed to believing in God, Tom practiced his faith by mentally devoting himself to the rules of the Catholic Church. He submitted to its authority. He recognized the sacraments as written, acknowledged the reasoning behind them, and chose to abide by them. As a natural part of this he went to Mass regularly and recognized Jesus Christ in the Eucharist and prayer.

Tom spent a great deal of time in prayer and meditation on God's presence. It helped him understand his purpose in life and gave him direction regarding what was right and wrong. If God was real and thus supernatural and superior to humanity, then by definition God's way had to be better than his own. He wanted to know what God's way was.

About a year before he died, Tom shared with me that he had been going to daily mass at a church near his office. It was something he felt compelled to do. He said he felt God had a message for him but he didn't know what it was. I was intrigued because Tom rarely spoke so openly about his faith. He said that he felt if he could spend more time in prayer and in church, then maybe he would be able to figure it out. I asked if he had any idea what it may be. He said, "No, but I know it will impact a great number of people, and it has something to do with the White House." (God must have had a good chuckle that day, because my response was, "He wants you to run for President!")

True to his Christian faith, Tom didn't just go to church and worship God, he chose to try to live daily in a way that was pleasing to Him. This meant having a clear understanding of what was right and wrong in God's eyes. Again, if God was God, then due to His superior nature, God's definition of right and wrong would be superior to that of mankind.

Tom had a deep love for our country and treasured the faith in God upon which it had been founded. It disturbed him greatly that many Americans had turned away from seeking God for their purpose in life. In addition, the decreasing focus on prayer also sorrowed him.

He saw huge repercussions for us as a nation for our growing lack of belief in a Sovereign God and increasing tendency for self-reliance. The emphasis in the media on who made the most money, acquired the most stuff, and gained the most visibility in the public eye (celebrity) was no measure of true success. What they promoted was a lie. It seemed to Tom that many were living increasingly under a misguided and ultimately unfulfilling philosophy which placed greater value on what they did for a living, what they owned, and how much money they had. He believed true fulfillment and joy was found by focusing on developing an innate goodness and love for others which would pour itself out in selfless acts of kindness and courage.

Where was the recognition in the media for all the lives well-lived through choices to love others by actions performed every day? It was as if those making the right choices were becoming more and more invisible in our society. In Tom's opinion, without God and His way of loving as the focal point in our society, our priorities were becoming more and more wrongly placed.

Tom also had been concerned deeply by the increasing disregard for basic morals. Morals demonstrate a respect for the dignity and value of every individual at a level much higher than our basic animalistic instincts. The indifference shown by much of the public to immoral acts committed and admitted to by high ranking officials in our government prior to 2001 was appalling. No one seemed to care anymore. As a country Tom saw us turning further and further away from the values which had made this country great and caused it to be so richly blessed for over 200 years.

Tom's faith additionally told him that work is good. It is a blessing. Work is to be embraced, not avoided. He saw self-discipline as a critical component of the process through which the personal growth comes so that you can later do what you will be called upon to do. He understood that there is a lot of truth to the slogan, "No pain, no gain". Tom wanted the gain enough that he disciplined himself to do whatever was necessary to achieve his goal.

His Values

Tom was adamant about the difference between right and wrong. He didn't believe in moral relativity. There was no such thing as "what's true for you is true and what's true for me is equally true". When people found ways to rationalize bad behavior, poor decisions, or a lack of self-discipline, it irritated him. And if you weren't sure or were unclear what was absolute right or wrong, then you hadn't given it enough thought.

Yet Tom simultaneously believed that everyone should have their own opinion. Each should stand up for what he or she believed. He hated it when people acted like weather vanes and changed their thoughts due to popular opinion. He encouraged people close to him to be clear on what their thoughts were and why they had them.

Tom used to say, "If you don't stand for something, you'll fall for anything." I loved that. There was such power and truth in those few words.

An honorable man, Tom impressed upon me that it was healthy to debate your beliefs. It was acceptable to try to persuade other people to think the way you did. In fact, it was even possible to do so without offending them. Tom believed that if you truly thought through your thoughts in order to know why you believe the way you do and if you were able to articulate your points well, then other people would be more apt to come over to your side.

Because Tom lived what he believed, when he spoke people listened. Chances were he had something to say that was well thought out and brilliantly formulated which they hadn't heard before.

Tom also taught me that it was all right not to be accepting of all things and all people. He believed it was okay not to be tolerant. Initially, this was a new concept for me. I had spent so much time in my life just accepting everyone for who they were. Tom challenged me to think differently.

At one point I accused him of being judgmental. To my surprise, he wasn't insulted at all. Instead, he laughed and agreed with me. "If we don't judge people," he said, "Then we lose the concept of right versus wrong and the moral fiber of our country begins to deteriorate." "If it's wrong, then it's wrong," he would say. "There are good opinions and there are poor ones. You don't have to be accepting of something you believe to be morally wrong."

Yet in the same instant, Tom also was abundantly compassionate. In his judgment, he didn't believe in hurting or harming other people just because you didn't agree with their morality. He didn't believe in discriminating against their rights as set forth by the Constitution. He simply believed it was all right to disagree with them and to stand up for your own beliefs.

Long before September 11th, Tom lived by principles which told him to stand up, stand firm, do something, and fight back for those things in which he believed.

Tom enjoyed celebrating life every day, rather than waiting for holidays. It was not uncommon to have a bottle of champagne and several toasts for no reason. For instance, on New Year's Eve it was our custom to go to bed at nine o'clock. Tom was very safety conscious. He thought it dangerous to be out on a night when people generally drank too much and acted imprudently.

He hated the aspect of what he called "commercial celebrations" in which we were obligated to give gifts, i.e., Mother's Day, Father's Day, Valentine's Day, etc. He reluctantly participated by giving gifts because he knew it was something I enjoyed, but he didn't like it.

In our home there were no New Year's resolutions. Tom believed that if changes in our lives needed to be made, they should be made immediately. No waiting for an artificial start date. If it was important, why wait for a certain day to start implementing plans?

In every decision he made, Tom used research and thought. Reading, discussing, and thinking were his passions. They benefited his manner of processing questions and issues which confronted him.

His Drive

Tom looked to make his life count in every regard. He worked tirelessly at a company whose purpose was to save lives. He was proud of his work and yet he was a devoted husband, father, son, brother, and friend. He didn't care about material things, but believed the children should have the very best in education and a mother to stay home with them.

Tom had the drive and motivation that allowed him to soar in the business world. Even though I felt guilty that part of why he went to work was to provide for us, I knew that his drive and motivation came from deep within. They had been with him since childhood. Regardless of us, I knew he would have worked just as hard and long.

My husband often joked that he would be just as happy hunting and fishing in the woods for his food. But in my heart of hearts, I knew this wasn't true. I knew that he wasn't the kind of man who would live a life without the drive and challenge and competition that came with his career. He thrived on this challenge. He always had.

Tom had so many dreams. Like his father, one day he wanted to be a teacher and influence the lives of our youth. He wanted to be a politician and shape our country's laws. He loved the French culture and dreamed of long family vacations in the south of France so we could become fluent in the language. He was excited about an upcoming hunting and fishing trip in Alaska. The list went on and on.

Passionate about reading and always learning more, Tom did not understand why everyone else didn't share the same passion. "Reading is the best way to improve yourself. If we don't continue to acquire knowledge, then we can't understand the world as it changes around us." In addition, "When trying to gain a new perspective or researching a topic, self-improvement may not be the goal, but it is the result."

"Turn off the television and pick up a book for a change," he would say. To make his point, a year into our marriage, he convinced me to get rid of the television for a period of time. Surprisingly, I found it to be positive. We spent a year "enriching our minds through good books and conversation". When we wanted entertainment, we turned on the radio. One of our favorites was listening to Garrison Keillor's program on Sunday afternoons.

Tom was always reading. His appetite was insatiable. He liked it when the two of us could read the same book at the same time and then discuss it – sort of our own mini book club. We rarely were successful because he seemed to have more time to read than I did, especially after the girls were born.

Tom also loved American history. He ravenously digested book after book about the American Wars and the generals who conducted them. He also loved presidential biographies. No doubt this reading strengthened his sense of patriotism for our country.

He marveled at the courage of the soldiers who fought at Gettysburg in the Civil War. Men, who knew they were going to meet their death, but fought anyway. More than once Tom told me that he wondered whether he had that kind of courage.

Deena L. Burnett
Built on a Strong Foundation

"Take courage and turn your troubles into material for spiritual progress." – St Francis de Sales

My first memory was the birth of my baby brother, Scotty. I was three years old in 1967. I remember Mom laying this tiny creature down on a bed. My face peered over his, staring as he made baby noises.

Startled, I asked, "What's that, Mom? What did he say? Do it again, baby."

My mom laughed and explained that babies couldn't speak.

I didn't care. "Can Scotty play?" I asked.

"No, no. He's too little to play with right now."

"Then can you take him back and get another one?"

Our family lived in a house Dad built for Mom on a cotton farm in Halley, Arkansas. Halley was a small farming community two hours southeast of Little Rock in the Mississippi Delta.

Our town had less than 60 people. Everyone knew each other, and we all went to the same Baptist Church. The church was the focal point of the community. All of the town's social activities took place there. There were cakewalks and boxed lunch auctions once a month to benefit the Homemaker's Club. Saturday afternoons were filled with softball and basketball games at the church community park and on

Sunday nights there were potluck dinners. Our family went to church twice every Sunday and once on Wednesday.

During the summer, my dad couldn't always make it because he had to work in the fields. What I remember most about him is that he could sing. Whether in church or under the shade of the tree in our front yard, he would often sing old gospel hymns to my brother and me. I usually tried to sing along with him, my brother would just listen.

I lived a simple, happy childhood, surrounded by family and friends who loved me. My grandparents lived close by, within walking distance. So did my aunts and uncles and most of my cousins on my Dad's side. Most of my mother's family lived in California.

Our family did everything together. My dad, his older brother and grandpa farmed together. We went to church together. We ate Sunday dinners together. We spent the holidays together. I saw my aunts, uncles, and grandparents as often as I saw my parents. They all played impressionable roles in my life. They lived what they believed, instilling early the importance of values such as honesty, integrity, love for your family and friends, and to be of service to those around you. I was taught to put God and country first in your life and that happiness was in giving and doing for others rather than receiving or having something done for you.

In particular my parents impressed upon me never to borrow things from others. If you couldn't afford it, then do without. They taught me there was value in not having everything. There was goodness in using what you had instead of always wanting more.

Sometimes I rode around with my dad in his Chevy pick-up truck. Every couple of years, he bought a new one. He had to. Life on the cotton farm wore them down pretty quick. He also loved to hunt. Even after a long day of farming in the fields, we often drove down by the levee along the Mississippi River or at the edge of the woods searching for deer. I always stood on the seat beside him and kept an eye out.

My best friend, Barbie, lived just down the road. My dad said we looked like Mutt and Jeff. I was tall and lanky. She was petite. It didn't matter. We were the same age and spent our days crawdad fishing on the bayou, taking pieces of bacon as bait and stringing up long sticks as fishing poles. We also used to sneak large red handled spoons from my grandma's kitchen and head for the cotton fields, trying to dig our way to China. If we got tired of doing that, we rode our bikes up and down the country roads, stopping every once in awhile to play on the backyard swing sets. There wasn't anything we didn't do together.

There was a downside to growing up in a small town, however. Everyone knew everyone else's business. Over and over my mother told me, "Your reputation, Deena. You have to be careful about the things you say and do. Otherwise sooner or later you will become the subject of gossip." This was a lesson which would serve me well later.

For the time being I just knew I didn't want to become the subject of gossip. I became acutely aware of the importance of what other people may think. I was an obedient child. I believed my parents knew what was best for me. If they told me to do something, I did it without question.

Though we lived in such a small town, my mom would save money all year long so we could enjoy an extensively planned trip once a year. She wanted us to experience life outside the Delta, so unlike most other families in the area, we took an annual vacation out of state. Every two years this trip took us to visit her family in the San Joaquin Valley of California. Since my dad didn't like to fly, we always drove, taking different routes each time so we could see different parts of the country. These trips alone exposed my brother and me to 11 different states. We saw the Grand Canyon and toured cities like San Francisco, Los Angeles, Phoenix, and Las Vegas. Wherever we traveled we did everything there was to do. The trips accomplished my mother's objective. With every year my realization grew that there was more to the world than southeast Arkansas, and I was hungry for more.

One Sunday after services when I was nine years old, I trailed my mother and father as usual to the minister at the back of the church. He was shaking everyone's hand and bidding them farewell. He took my hand and looked right at me. Then he looked at my parents and said, "I don't know what God has in store for Deena, but I feel like it's something that will affect a lot of people in a great way." What the minister said frightened me, but as time went on I disregarded it as something he must have said to please my parents. Years later, as I sought to pick up the pieces after 9/11, his words would come back to encourage me to be strong and step forward.

My life seemed idyllic. These early years gave me strong roots of faith and family, which would sustain me through many coming storms.

The first storm hit when I was fourteen. My parents divorced. In the 1970's in southeast Arkansas no one divorced. It was a tragedy that struck our entire small community. Adults and children alike cried and hugged me as if someone in our family had died.

I didn't know what to do with my feelings. I tried to understand, but failed. I had a boyfriend at school; certainly I thought I was old enough to understand relationships. I thought I knew what love was. But I could not comprehend why my mother didn't love my father anymore.

With Mom seeming confused, Dad sad, and my eleven year old brother angry about the divorce, what emotion was left for me? I felt like I had to be strong for everyone, so even though I was upset, I never shared my feelings with anyone.

It was during this difficult time that God gave me a special gift of comfort and encouragement, which would help me for many years to come. I was introduced to Dr. Robert Schuller's book, *Move Ahead With Possibility Thinking*. Dr. Schuller was an evangelical preacher who had begun his ministry going door-to-door recruiting people to attend his church. Operating on less than a shoestring, he started his church by using a drive-in theater during daylight hours where he preached from the rooftop of the concession stand. By the time I was 14, he had created a strong church community in Southern California housed in the famous Crystal Cathedral and had become a well-known televangelist with a worldwide audience who faithfully tuned in every week.

His book helped me find purpose when the life I had known as a child was falling apart around me.

I was struggling with finding my place within the framework of my new family situation both at home and in the community. The words in *Move Ahead With Possibility Thinking* helped me look at things in a completely new light. It taught me how to think positively in bad situations. I learned that you may not have control over the circumstances that occur in your life, but you do have a choice in how you react to them.

To give me hope and inspiration and help get me through, I took phrases from this book such as, "Problems are guidelines, not stop signs" and "Each adversity hides a possibility" and pasted them to my bedroom mirror.

After the divorce, Mom moved to the nearby town of McGehee. Dad remained in our family home in Halley. Scotty and I lived with him on the weekends. But for me any semblance of childhood had ended with their divorce. At Dad's I became the lady of the house. I stocked the pantry, cleaned, did the laundry, and cooked the meals. Responsibilities that had been Mom's were suddenly mine. It was overwhelming at first, but in time I adjusted. The house began to feel like mine and I took pride in my actions.

Now on her own, Mom began to treat me like an adult. She shared personal feelings with me that I didn't necessarily want to know. Where I had relied on her my whole life as resilient and able to handle anything, I now saw her in all her humanity – vulnerable and subject to confusion and unhappiness just like anyone else. Formerly confident and strong, it was odd to see her in situations where she didn't always know what direction to turn or what decision was best. She asked me for advice, but all I could tell her was to follow her heart.

While in high school my horizons were expanded once again. Both Dad and Mom remarried. Before long my step-mom became pregnant and gave birth to a baby sister, named Kara. I thought she was the most beautiful baby I had ever seen. But I was also human and when more and more of Dad's time and energy seemed to go into caring for his new family, even though it was wrong for me to feel jealous, I was.

Kara was born with a deficient heart and needed a life-saving operation. She was so small and young, the doctors said she would need to be at least four months old to undergo the surgery. Two weeks before she turned four months old, I was playing in a high school basketball game and noticed my Dad was not there. He always came to my games. This was the first he had ever missed. I didn't know what to think, but I was certain it had something to do with that baby. I was upset. Why couldn't he be at the game with me? I felt less important and valued again. But after the game I learned that Kara had died that afternoon. My Baptist upbringing made me feel like it was my fault, that somehow I had played a part in the baby's death. I thought that if you didn't live your life just right, God would punish you. I wondered if perhaps God had taken Kara away because of my jealousy. I felt like this was my punishment. Healing took a long, long time.

Just seven months later, a few days before my sixteenth birthday, my grandma died. Her death was especially difficult for me because I loved her as much as my mother. We had been very, very close. I didn't understand what I was doing wrong. I was trying so hard to do everything right. I was captain of the girl's basketball team, a cheerleader, and a member of the National Honor Society, a good kid with good grades. What was missing? I spent a lot of time thinking about what makes a person happy and referring back to Dr. Schuller's book. I knew happiness came from inside, I just didn't know how to pull it out. My friends helped me hold life together.

Systematically everything I had held onto as true and real was being pulled out from under me. This was compounded when right before I entered my senior year of high school, my mom's husband took a job in Pensacola, Florida. It was only an eight hour drive away, but it seemed half-way around the world.

Where in Halley I seemingly had had it all, now I was frightened, intimidated, and lonely. After coming from a close-knit community with a total population of 60 people, I was in a new school with 502 students in the senior class alone. It was more people than I had ever seen in one place in my entire life.

Unwittingly and uncomfortably I was learning that life is about transitions, and I was being put in a position time and again of having to put Dr. Schuller's teachings into use. I could not control the different course my life had taken, but I could choose how I reacted to it. I made it through my senior year, but the day after graduation I moved back to the house in which I grew up to spend summer in Halley before going off to college.

I was raised on the belief that to be better educated meant to have more opportunities. I was accepted into Southern Methodist University in Dallas. The school's tuition was more than we could afford, but my parents were determined to try to make it work. Freshmen were required to live on campus, but I had applied late for room and board. The regular dormitory rooms were full, so I was given what seemed to be a large storage closet as it had no window. It was also located next to the elevator, so it was rather noisy.

My roommate's name was Nancy, and she and I were worlds apart. She thought I was a naïve back country girl, and I wasn't sure what to think of her. She spoke with her hands and had brought a tough-guy accent with her from Philadelphia. Initially she and her friends were using our dorm room for purposes I thought were wrong. At first I wasn't sure what to do. I called my dad and asked his advice. He said I should report her and that he would come pick me up and bring me home. That panicked me. I didn't want to leave, so I had to find a way to handle it. After spending my first night at SMU on the couch in the dorm lounge, I mustered up the courage to confront her. I presented that she was putting us both at risk for flagrantly breaking dorm rules. And though she probably thought I was over-reacting, she respected my position and stopped.

Just as she presented urban 1980's culture shock to me, my rural southern background was a source of amusement for her. Though she saw me as prim and proper, always careful to make sure my tennis shoes were white, clothes pressed and hair curled, she made fun of my accent and anytime I went home she wanted to know what was going to be on the menu. She couldn't believe we actually ate wild game. She especially thought it hilarious that we occasionally ate squirrels, which she, in her northern way, called rodents.

The entire SMU experience was a sort of culture shock for me. Again, my world was broadening. Where I had been raised to work with what I had and be content as well as grateful, I found myself surrounded by privileged children who were academically bright, but socially less mature. Many of them had gone to some of the best high schools and boarding schools in the country. They had a lot of money and spent it on designer clothes and foreign cars. They did not value work the same as I had been raised. Some of them even had their dorm rooms decorated by interior designers with custom draperies and bedspreads. And they amazed me how they could party non-stop yet still get up in the morning, get to class, and make good grades.

Partying was not in my schedule. To make ends meet, I was one of the few students who had to work part time. Classes began at 8 a.m. and ended at 2 p.m. Then I would go to work until 8 p.m., racing back to the dorm to study until midnight. For the first time in my life, I struggled academically. I used mountains of coffee to sustain me.

After three semesters at SMU I moved back home and transferred to a smaller school, the University of Arkansas at Monticello. As much as I had wanted to stay at SMU, I realized it was way too much of a financial strain on my dad. The farm was struggling and he was having a difficult time paying the tuition. Had I pushed, he probably would have found a way, but I felt it was too selfish of me to ask.

Monticello was a different college experience all together. It was not a metropolitan city like Dallas. The football team didn't have players with national name recognition like Eric Dickerson or Craig James.

After one semester at Monticello I had completed my general education units and decided to transfer to Northeast Louisiana University. I had wanted to be a home economics teacher, but Mom encouraged me to do something she thought would be more fun, like a radio broadcaster. I wasn't sure about being a broadcaster, but since it did sound exciting, I identified Northeast Louisiana University to be the nearest school which offered the communications degree I would need.

All I cared about was graduating and getting my degree. It was back to the old balancing act of working and going to school at the same time.

At NLU I was able to earn 75 percent of the tuition by working while I went to school. My parents did whatever they could to help with the rest. Which degree I earned wasn't as important to them as just graduating from college. All of my parents worked hard and made sacrifices to make sure that the finances were in place for me to complete school.

To finish more quickly and minimize expenses I took as many credits as I could. Most semesters I averaged 18 to 21 hours. My last semester I took 27. I studied and worked all the time. At one point I held two jobs and had 21 credits. Some days I would be so busy I would forget to eat and actually passed out on campus twice from exhaustion and lack of food. I just had to get through.

December 1985 I reached my goal and graduated. It had taken me three and a half years to work my way through college. I felt relief at being done and regretted only that I had been unable to earn the better grades of which I was capable because I had been stretched so thin.

Mom came up from Pensacola and Dad traveled from Halley to be with me for the ceremony. I can still remember the uneasiness of having both my parents under the same roof. Even as an adult, my life was still burdened by their choice to divorce.

I landed my first position at a radio station in Fort Walton Beach, Florida, doing local news reporting and anchoring the radio during the morning drive time. I moved into a little beach house on Pensacola Beach and enjoyed living life on my own.

After a year, I was ready for a change. The radio station paid so little that I still had to work two other jobs just to make ends meet. I was tired all the time and frustrated that at the age of 24 I still never had time or money for fun. And I wanted to travel. It seemed the easiest way to accomplish my objective would be to work for an airline and so

I went to the airport and applied to every airline that had an application available. My world was about to broaden greatly.

Chapter Three

Two Lives Inextricably Intertwined

"Make my joy complete by being like-minded, having the same love, being one in spirit and purpose." – The Bible, Philippians 2:2

Introductions

My first emotion when I met Tom Burnett was annoyance. But it wasn't his fault.

Three years after graduating from college in April 1989 I began working for Delta Airlines and moved to Atlanta, Georgia. My roommate was Camille Bowler. She spoke French and was also a flight attendant. Camille gave new meaning to the word outgoing.

To celebrate completion of our training we decided to have a girls' night out at a local pub. There were 15 of us to meet for happy hour. Having just flown in from a trip, I was late and the last to arrive. My hair was still wet from showering.

When I walked in, I noticed Camille was talking in her animated fashion to this guy, who she introduced as Tom Burnett. I responded politely and then turned my focus to one of our friends. I knew flight attendant scheduling was trying to reach her. Since she was staying temporarily with us, she needed a ride back to the apartment, so I took her.

Forty-five minutes later when we returned, I was a little more put together. My hair was curled, my face touched up, and I was dressed in evening clothes. To my annoyance, Camille was still talking with this guy. It was supposed to be a girl's night out and her focus was somewhere else. My irritation level escalated markedly when out of the blue she invited him to join us when we decided to leave the pub and go downtown. He said yes.

We drove separately as we all headed to a nightclub. The entire way there Camille talked about the car Tom drove. She was impressed. A nice car meant a good job. This meant the guy could afford to take her to nice restaurants. She figured at a minimum it would be fun to get to know him. She talked on and on feeding my frustration. What right had she had to include this guy in our evening?

We were at the club less than 20 minutes before Camille ran off and completely ignored Tom. Now I felt a little sorry for him – although one guy in the company of 15 women – he didn't have it that bad.

I decided to talk with him. He seemed nice. The conversation was good. We danced a couple of times. Before the night was over Camille resurfaced and started talking to him again. To my amazement, when we left she gave him a list of all of our phone numbers. Ours was at the top. He had not asked her for any of them, but politely thanked her and tucked the note in his pocket. With no reason to think otherwise, I thought that was the end of that.

A week later I heard a message on our answering machine. It was Tom. He invited both Camille and me over to his apartment for dinner. He said he would cook. Even though the message was for both of us, I felt Camille should return the call. This was a relationship she had initiated and pursued, not I.

After a few days I asked if she had returned the call. She was nonchalant. Not yet, but she intended to. Another day passed and my Southern manners were getting the best of me. The call needed to be returned. Finally Camille passed it off on me. "He liked you better anyway. You call him." So I did.

I explained Camille wasn't available for dinner but I would welcome it. He immediately impressed me with his decorum. If Camille couldn't come, he suggested we meet at a local restaurant. Since I didn't know him well yet, it would probably be much too uncomfortable otherwise for me to come to his apartment. I very much appreciated his thoughtfulness.

Dinner out was strange. Though neither of us really remembered what the other looked like, but when we saw each other at the restaurant we recognized one another immediately. Tom greeted me with a kiss on the cheek, which startled me. It seemed so forward. As it turned out, he had done it because he thought it was a Southern custom for friends to greet in this manner. Being a Minnesotan in Atlanta and true to who he was, he had been trying to do the "right" thing.

Dinner was ordered, served, and eaten in the first 45 minutes, but we sat there for six hours talking. If the restaurant hadn't closed we would have stayed longer. Establishing a pattern which would last for our entire relationship, Tom did most of the talking. But I didn't mind. He was interesting and what he had to say was frequently thought-provoking. He spoke with great love and loyalty of his family in Bloomington, Minnesota. His father, mother, and sisters were very important to him. I learned about his stint at the Air Force Academy during the summer of 1981 after completing high school. He had not wanted to go, but it was important to his father. Tom Sr. was a high school English teacher and Korean War veteran. Although Tom completed his basic training, he did not continue. He didn't agree with the air of superiority held by the upper classmen and how they treated the cadets.

We covered all the controversial subjects that first night. We talked about the struggle of women in the workplace: choosing a career versus raising children at home. He told me stories of his sister and the difficulties she had in making those decisions. He asked what I thought of women playing professional sports with their ranks growing. We even entered the "forbidden" zone and talked about politics and religion. Interestingly, in the years to come these would become two of our favorite topics of discussion.

Tom was obviously very bright. The more I listened the more I learned.

When it finally came time to go, Tom paid for the meal, which confused me. I thought we just were going to be friends and should each pay half. Tom wouldn't hear of it.

A week later he called and asked me out to dinner again. This time there was no confusion. I knew it was a date. He picked me up at the apartment, and we went to an Italian restaurant. Once more Tom did most of the talking, but I didn't mind. Suddenly while telling me stories about his childhood, like sticking up for other kids in junior high and camping and hunting in the summers with his dad, Tom reached up to the overhanging light fixture, unscrewed the light bulb, and tossed it over his shoulder. It smashed on the floor. Throughout the entire antic he continued to talk, never once even changing his tone of voice. When he noticed the alarmed look on my face he just smiled and said, "I'm just trying to create an atmosphere here and that light wasn't helping."

I giggled. There was spontaneity and fun in Tom Burnett I liked. Even though it seemed like an odd gesture, I found it strangely romantic. "This is not just a nice guy," I thought to myself. "There's more to him than I'm seeing."

At the end of the night, he politely kissed me on the cheek and left.

The next day I called my mom and told her about him.

"Deena, this sounds serious," she replied.

"Yes, I know. I'm going to marry him."

"What? Are you in love with him?"

"No, but I'm going to be."

"Are you sure?"

"Yes, we're going to get married. But don't tell him because he doesn't know it yet."

Courtship

I'm sure Mom didn't think I was serious, but I was. Suddenly I knew what everyone meant when they would say, "You'll know when you meet the right guy. It can't be explained, you'll just know." There was just something about Tom Burnett.

Even though in certain ways Tom was a deep thinker and a complex man, for some reason it was easy for me to get to know him. I didn't feel like I had to try. I just listened and who he was became intimate and comfortable for me.

Though different in many ways, the foundation upon which our character and values were built was similar. I liked how important his family was to him. I liked how his faith in God gave him his direction and purpose. I liked how we both believed in the existence of true right and wrong in a world which more and more was emphasizing relativity.

I also found him incredibly charming. He was a gentleman in every regard, and I enjoyed his ongoing acts of chivalry. He would walk around the car to open my door, pull out chairs for me to sit, stand when I stood, and only sit after I had sat down.

Though I was frequently the listener in our conversations, I could tell early on that Tom was fond of me and it felt good. Tom genuinely was interested in everything I did and said.

The freshness of our relationship never seemed to end and like most couples newly in love, we were always excited to see each other. Anytime Tom picked me up at my apartment he brought flowers. Mostly they were traditional flowers like red or pink roses, but occasionally he would bring daisies.

Even though Tom and I were close in age, to me he seemed so much more knowledgeable about the world and how it works. He worked for a company called Calictek, a manufacturer of dental implants. As a sales director, he traveled around the world. When he returned from trips to Hong Kong, Tokyo, and Seoul with stories about his travels, it re-ignited in me the desire to see more of the world as well. I wanted my own experiences and eventually signed up to do international flights to Europe out of Atlanta.

Tom traveled Monday through Friday. Since I was a reserve flight attendant, I worked three days on and one off. So, though it might seem somewhat ironic, we spent most of our courtship on airplanes. It wasn't unusual for me to work an all-nighter from Los Angeles to Atlanta, get off the plane at 5:30a.m., and then hop on another plane just to have breakfast with him in Orlando.

Every week we compared travel schedules to see when we could get together again. As a result, much of our dating took place in different cities across the country. We met in airports and stayed in touch through voice mail. He called me every day to let me know where he was. I let him know which cities I was flying through. If we were ever in the same city, we tried to meet for a meal. At first Tom was flying Eastern Airlines, but then he switched to Delta. Sometimes I would check his flight itinerary through the computer and leave love notes for him at different gates. (Years later I found some of the notes he had saved at the bottom of his briefcase or suitcase and even after we married, I continued to put new little notes in his suit jacket pocket.)

After three months of dating, Tom starting asking what I thought about marriage. He wanted to know how I saw my future. How many children did I want? Where did I want to live? Did I want to work? What would be my ideal situation? This was very typical for Tom. He wanted as much information as possible. He was very good at decision-making and his ability to gather and sort through information was usually the reason.

I was asking questions, too, but I let him take the lead. I wanted marriage to be his idea. I didn't push him, though I wanted to. I was having such a great time dating him, I kept telling myself to be patient and enjoy being with him. I didn't put demands on him, which may be why we dated for as long as we did.

We had dated for two and a half years by the time he got around to proposing. Tom was living in San Diego while Atlanta was still my home. We were at his apartment around three o'clock in the afternoon. I was scheduled to fly out the next day, so he had left work early so we could be together. When he grabbed a bottle of champagne out of the refrigerator and plopped it down on the coffee table, it seemed out of character. He sat down next to me on the sofa and said, "Deena, we've been talking about getting married for some time."

"Yes."

"So what do you think?"

I was puzzled. I wasn't sure if he was actually proposing. Many times while we had been dating he had asked me if he proposed whether I would say yes. "No one wants to ask someone to marry him and have her say, no," he would say. This always made me laugh, but I never answered him.

"Are you asking me to marry you?"

"Yes."

I didn't respond, trying to figure out if he was serious.

Then he said, "I'm not going to ask a second time."

Immediately, I said, "Yes. So are we engaged now?"

"Yes, we're engaged."

"Okay then, call your parents." I knew if he called them, then he was serious.

Tom picked up the phone and as he dialed the number I became so excited I thought I would explode. I was actually going to be his wife! As he told them we were engaged, I sat there with my mouth open realizing that what I had known since our second date finally was going to happen.

He placed two boxes in front of me. I opened the first one. It was a huge diamond ring, only the diamond looked more like glass. He was making goofy faces, shaking his head back and forth, letting me know he knew it wasn't real. I opened the second one. It was a sapphire ring with diamonds on each side. I realized immediately that it wasn't real either. I looked at him wondering what was up. He said, "I wanted to propose today, but didn't have a ring. So I went downtown to this little costume jewelry shop and the woman there gave me these two rings to have you try on. I thought you could wear one of these until we could choose a real one."

He was convinced I had to go with him to choose the engagement ring. I knew he had been shopping for a year and yet still had not decided on a style. As was his way, he had been collecting information to make the best decision. He had become an expert on diamonds and done all the necessary research and yet before me sat two $8 rings. I laughed and chose the ring with the big glass diamond and told him I wanted the decision on the actual ring to be his. I didn't care about the ring. He could have given me a big cigar band and I would have cherished it. I just wanted to spend the rest of my life with him.

But at the moment of my greatest joy when I said, yes, to his proposal, the thought dropped into my mind that we would never grow old together. It was as if God was already preparing me for what was to come. I knew and God knew that something was going to happen. I sensed it would be something significant. God knew that the time would come when I would have to rely on Him alone for my strength. Before the sound of my 'yes' had finished being uttered, I heard God whispering to me, "Really think about this, Deena. Prepare yourself. You can do this." *Do what? Prepare for what? I have no idea what You're talking about!*

Marriage

Tom gave me a real diamond engagement ring the night before my first bridal shower. I loved that he had waited until then. His family and friends were going to be there, and he didn't want them to see the fake ring on my finger.

At first we couldn't decide where to get married. Tom wanted a Catholic wedding. I wanted to get married in my hometown Baptist church. The plan was to get married in my church with a Catholic priest. Since there was difficulty in having that approved by the Catholic Diocese, we used a small Catholic church near my hometown.

We were married the first weekend after Easter on April 25, 1992, seven months after he proposed. Tom chose his dad as his best man and my step-sister Kristen was my maid of honor. Monsignor Joe, a family friend of the Burnett's from Iowa performed the ceremony making it intimate and memorable. We spent our honeymoon in Aruba.

Naturally, in the beginning, marriage was an adjustment. We were both in our late twenties and used to living our own lives without having to be accountable to anyone. The commitment of marriage changed our relationship in two ways. First, it made it permanent. Tom and I both believed the commitment of marriage was forever. Secondly, we were now responsible to one another.

We lived in a small apartment in Carlsbad, California and both worked long hours. We lived frugally. Rather than accumulate stuff and more stuff, we had one goal in mind: to save enough to enable me to stay home once we had children and save for their future.

Our budget was $100 per week for groceries, gas, and entertainment. I managed the money. I bought in bulk at wholesale warehouses and discount groceries to save money. It was not unusual for me to come home with something like ten pounds of carrots, twenty pounds of potatoes, five pounds of onions, and ten pounds of chicken. Anything we could make with those ingredients we did. After having vegetable or chicken soup for seemingly the forty-third night in a row, all we could do was laugh. At the end of each week, if there was any money left, I put it in a jar hoping there would soon be enough to treat ourselves to a dinner out.

In contrast, many of the people at work who reported to Tom as well as our friends lived in large expensive homes with expensive furniture. Tom believed practicing self-denial now would be valuable later in our lives. This coincided with the values with which I had been raised, so we continued to live on our budget saving every dime we could.

Tom and I didn't argue often and like most couples we developed our own little way of working out differences. There was really no point in arguing with Tom. He was a fair and reasonable person, with strong opinions that were well thought out. He always won the argument and more times than not, could bring you around to his way of thinking. At the very least you would walk away doubting your own position on the issue.

When something became an issue, I listened patiently as he stormed around, sometimes resembling a trial attorney building his case, even raising his voice from time to time. Although I disagreed with him, I wouldn't let him know. That is, until the next day. After a good night's rest he was usually in a different frame of mind and I could catch him off guard. In the end, I usually got my way. He would laugh and say I was the only person in the world to whom he would give in.

We celebrated our first anniversary by vacationing at my mom's condo in Perdido Key, Florida. We had become much more comfortable with the commitment of marriage and marveled every day how our relationship continued to improve. We also felt we were ready to have children.

We wanted five. I called it a basketball team. Tom called it the best of the football team.

But it wasn't so easy. After a year and then two I was still having difficulty conceiving. We went to see a fertility specialist and after one month on fertility drugs I was finally pregnant.

I couldn't wait to surprise Tom with the news. When I picked up Tom at the airport I pretended everything was as usual. However, when we arrived home, I had posted a note on the front door for him to find which read, "The quarterback for your football team arrives in nine months." When he opened the door and went inside, he was engulfed by a sea of pink and blue balloons. Tears welled up in his eyes and he had the biggest smile on his face. We toasted with a bottle of sparkling apple cider and then said a prayer. We thanked God for His blessing. So many times over the past several years we had prayed for a child. We felt like God's hand was upon us. Our prayers had been answered.

That weekend I flew my last trip as a flight attendant. Tom and I decided it wasn't worth taking any unnecessary risks while I was expecting.

Chapter Four

A Quiet, Happy Suburban Life

"Practice in life what you pray for and God will give it to you more abundantly." – E.B. Pusey

Not too many weeks into the pregnancy I realized I was bleeding. I began to cry and at that instant the telephone rang. It was Tom. "I had this feeling something was wrong."

"Yes," I answered. "I'm bleeding and I don't know what's wrong. I'm afraid I'm having a miscarriage."

Within five minutes Tom was home. In transit, he had called the doctor, who told him to bring me into the clinic immediately. Always the gentleman and a concerned family man, Tom reclined the car seat as far as it would go so that I could lie down. At the clinic they performed an ultrasound. To our relief, the pregnancy appeared fine.

"How many babies are you having?" the nurse asked.

"What?" I said.

She began counting, "One, two, three, four….no wait."

"How many are there?" said Tom.

"Oh my mistake, let me start over," responded the nurse.

There were actually three fetuses, but one wasn't developing. That's why I was bleeding. We were going to have twins. We were elated.

I was put on bed rest for the first trimester. Tom stopped traveling and waited on me hand and foot. Every morning before work he made me breakfast. At noon he came home and brought me lunch. Then in the evening he cooked dinner.

I carried the twins full term and had a C-section. In six minutes, we had two beautiful daughters. I watched Tom holding the girls. He gave one of them sugar water because she had low blood sugar. He looked so happy. We both were.

Halley Elizabeth and Madison Margaret were born on May 16, 1996 – the fourth year of our marriage. We had wanted their names to mean something, so in true Tom Burnett fashion we had poured over our family trees looking for names we could agree on. Halley was named after my hometown in Arkansas. Elizabeth was a family name. Tom chose the name Madison after my great grandfather. I persuaded him to use Margaret, which was his grandmother's name. That same afternoon Tom left the hospital and returned with medals inscribed with names of Catholic saints for the girls. When he was an infant he had been given a medal of St. Thomas Aquinas, which he had always cherished and wore around his neck. He gave Halley a St. Elizabeth medal and Madison received St. Margaret.

Two years after his death I learned that St. Elizabeth Seton and St. Margaret were the patron saints of bereaved children.

In August 1996 when the twins were three months old, Tom took a new job in San Francisco with Thoratec, a medical device company. His travel schedule picked up and he was gone Monday through Friday. I was left at home alone with two colicky newborns who cried all the time. Complicating matters further, Madison had a club foot that required extra care for its weekly cast change. I struggled to get on top of things emotionally.

I was feeling housebound, isolated, and was suffering from an identity crisis. Before children I had been independent and mobile. Now, even though I was doing exactly that which we had planned, it was a huge adjustment being stuck at home with two babies. If I wasn't contributing money to the family, then what was I contributing? Changing diapers and mopping up spit didn't seem to have the value I thought it would. Our society values people so much based on what they do to earn a living, that if I wasn't a flight attendant I didn't know who I was anymore. I was hardly sleeping and felt isolated. Taking care of the girls took every ounce of energy I had left. Not only that, but I was 60 pounds heavier and I didn't know anyone in our neighborhood. All my friends lived in Los Angeles where I had worked.

So when the twins cried, I cried. What a sight to have the three of us on the sofa crying all day long. (I later learned that this behavior is normal for mothers of twins.)

In late 1996 we moved to the suburban community of San Ramon, about 45 minutes east from San Francisco, and we were able to buy our first house. House hunting in the San Francisco Bay Area was challenging to say the least. At that time, houses sold after an average of three days on the market, frequently at a price above the asking price. At first we had tried home shopping the traditional way. Tom had selected two or three for me to come look at, then we scheduled for me to fly up and see. But by the time I could make flight arrangements, pack the bags, and get the babies to the airport, the houses would have sold. So we opted for a house in a new development, where we could make the decision to purchase based on floor plan and architectural drawings.

When the twins turned one year old in May 1997, I learned I was pregnant again. Tom was so very happy when I told him. And while I was happy, too, I was so tired I started to cry. We both had a good laugh.

Anna Clare was born February 24, 1998. While I was in the hospital room, holding my newborn baby, my mom innocently commented, "Well, I guess you'll have to have a fourth baby so Tom can have his son."

"No, Mom. God isn't going to give us a son," I said without thinking.

"Why not?"

"God knows I can't raise Tom's son by myself," I said, not having any idea where these thoughts were coming from.

"What are you talking about," she asked.

"Tom's not going to be here to raise his children. He's going to be in a plane crash."

My mom dismissed my words as post-partum confusion and changed the subject. But going forward I remembered these words which I had spoken and they went deep within me. I did not allow them to spoil the increasing joy I felt in my life with Tom and the girls. But especially when Tom left on business trips, there was a deep sense of foreboding in me and even a little fear as I wondered if it would be the last time I saw him.

Tom and I actually talked about the possibility of him dying periodically. Though it didn't make sense, he also had long thought that he and I would not be growing old together and that our separation would be caused by death, not divorce. No matter how hard he tried, he couldn't seem to get past it. In his safety conscious way, he began to take precautions to protect the girls. For instance, after awhile he no longer wanted us to fly together on the same plane. He did not want to take the chance of the girls losing both their parents in one blow.

Again, it was as if God was preparing me, preparing us, for that which was to come.

With the birth of Anna Clare there was also a transition that occurred for me internally. My identity crisis was over. I became very secure and happy in who I was. I was the wife of Tom Burnett and the mother of three wonderful young girls, all under the age of two. This was the life for which we had prayed. I had come to understand the value of my role and I was finally able to embrace it wholeheartedly and joyfully.

I was generally a very happy person and always had been.

At church I became involved in a women's program called Ministry of Mothers Sharing (MOMS). It was and is a curriculum-based program designed by a nun in Arizona for mothers with young children. MOMS examines everyday spirituality through self-discovery and prayer in a group setting which lends to the development of a solid network of friends in the church during a period of life when women can otherwise feel isolated and alone. Taking the MOMS class helped me focus on what my relationship with God really meant. I was blessed to learn to recognize God's grace-filled moments for me in everyday occurrences. Each of us in the class came from different walks in life. Diverse experiences had brought us there, so each of us had something to offer the others. Getting to know them got me involved in different aspects of the community. We were able to provide many different resources to each other. For me, these connections were even more important because I was so far away from family. The friendships formed with other MOMS participants became my new family network.

Meanwhile Tom was climbing the corporate ladder at Thoratec. His travels spanned the globe, from Europe to Japan. In 1999 he was named Senior Vice President and Chief Operating Officer. He was one of the best at what he did and always in demand for work at other companies. But he turned down many opportunities because he enjoyed working with his boss, Keith Grossman. Tom and Keith had been friends for almost two decades, virtually twice as long as I had known Tom. They had worked together at three different companies over the years. And while it was Tom's ultimate goal to run his own company at some point, he was in no hurry to leave working for Keith at Thoratec. At his relatively young age, Tom assumed that he would still have many opportunities to run his own company in years to come.

Tom rarely talked about work at home. Home was his haven, his family, his focus.

Saturdays were spent at the Pacific Ocean on the beach, which was approximately 30 minutes west of where we lived. It was the one place we could take the children where they could run around freely and enjoy themselves. Our joy was watching them and playing in the sand with them. As a year or two went by and they grew older, we had picnics, played Frisbee, and flew kites. It didn't matter the temperature or time of year.

During the summer we went to concerts in the park. The children played in the grass while Tom and I sat on a blanket, listening to music and sipping red wine.

For time alone, Tom and I would hire a babysitter for Friday or Saturday night. We had dinner out or saw a movie, but rarely did both.

We didn't want to be away from the children for more than two or three hours. About twice per year when my mother visited, we went into San Francisco to have dinner with friends. Mom was always a great babysitter.

Like my dad, Tom loved the outdoors. The year the twins were born we bought some hunting land in Wisconsin. The land also had an old farmhouse on it, which Tom used for lodging when he visited. About five times a year he made the trip to the farmhouse, working around the place and making repairs. He would walk the property and through the woods, scoping out game. This was his way of relaxing.

Camping seemed like it would be a natural offshoot of his love of outdoors and provided for "a fun family excursion." It took me a long time to persuade Tom to go camping the first time. If we were going to go camping, then it had to be what Tom called "real" camping. This meant wide-open wilderness. No state parks. To his way of thinking we would need to rough it in a tent, catch our own food, and no showers would be allowed. It took me awhile to convince him otherwise.

Making the Right Choices in the Midst of That Which We Can't Control

The year 2000 brought with it a great deal of stress to our young family. For two years, Halley had a horrible cough and an acute lack of energy. We had taken her to doctor after doctor on average of once every two weeks during this time and were told that she had everything from a cold or allergies or asthma to "simply does not know how to cough." Taking her back and forth to the hospital, trying to get a proper diagnosis was tiresome and frustrating. Finally we found a team of doctors who were willing to look further. She was tested for cystic fibrosis and the test came back positive.

Tom was in Boston when I received the test results. Because he traveled so much we were always in touch by phone. When I told him the news, there was absolute silence on the other end of the line. I quickly began to reassure him that I was certain she didn't have that fatal disease and not to worry. I would take her to another doctor to test again. I was sure this was a mistake. But when he finally spoke, it was as if the wind had been knocked out of him, "I'm coming home on the next flight. I'll call you from the airport."

I was stunned. I knew he was on a critical business trip. He couldn't just drop everything and leave, but he did. Family first. The right choice.

The two weeks that followed were the most heart wrenching we had ever experienced. We went through sessions with doctors to discuss treatment. Meanwhile she was tested for various potential complications which could occur due to cystic fibrosis. It was recommended that we have the two other girls tested, too, since it was a genetic disease.

Tom coped by doing what he always did, assimilating as much information as he could so he could make the best decision in light of circumstances, which appeared out of his control. He spent countless hours researching cystic fibrosis on the Internet and read everything he could get his hands on. He placed phone calls and shipped Halley's medical records to doctors all over the United States, Europe, and Japan.

Finally the third test for cystic fibrosis showed a negative result. Halley was diagnosed with something utterly treatable and her health immediately began to improve. The doctors apologized. Evidently the lab must have made mistakes with her first two samples. It was just days before Thanksgiving. We had so much for which to be thankful. It would be a celebration of genuine gratitude and prayer.

Tom and I agreed that we would never allow ourselves to forget the torment we experienced in believing our child had a fatal disease. We were humbled by and respectful of all parents who were living with that reality on a daily basis.

I remember when the ordeal was over Tom said, "Let's learn from this."

He wanted to ensure he made a difference in someone else's life. The thought of losing one or all of our children helped realign our priorities. He began taking more of his vacation time instead of working through it. He intended to join a men's organization for volunteering. We gave regular contributions to the Cystic Fibrosis Foundation and both of us became more involved at church. Besides my participating in Ministry of Moms Sharing, I looked after children in the church nursery and volunteered at different fundraising events. We tried to spend as much time together as a family as possible.

2001 found us both busy and happy. The girls were growing and expanding in their interests and abilities which pleased Tom greatly. Four and a half year olds Halley and Madison learned to ride their bicycles without training wheels. They took French lessons and ballet, and played in the predominantly boys' T-ball league. They learned how to swim. Three year old Anna Clare started participating in the Kumon math learning program. Tom was so proud.

Tom's job was going well. Thoratec was in a multi-million dollar negotiation to acquire New Jersey-based Thermocardio Systems, a competitor who had a product line that would complement theirs. This required Tom to travel quite a bit back and forth to the East Coast. Thermocardio had offices in Boston and New Jersey.

I was excitedly house hunting. We sat down with a realtor and began making plans to buy a dream home. We had outgrown our current home. We wanted more space for the girls both inside and outside, and yearned for a larger yard.

Halley's health continued to improve.

I kept busy both with the girls and supporting their activities. I was a room mom at their preschool and constantly planned social activities in and out of school so the moms and children could get to know each other better. We often hosted them in our home.

It was only January, but we began to talk more in earnest about our children's future education. In the fall Halley and Madison would be ready for kindergarten and the private schools application deadlines were pending. If at all possible, we wanted them to have a Christian education. While academics were foremost, we also believed it was important for them to continue learning the values at school that were being instilled at home – something a public school education could not provide. We filled out applications for our Catholic school and other Christian schools in the area and went to interviews. Tom juggled his schedule to accommodate the application process.

Tom and I agreed the girls should be well-educated. He believed that smart people made better decisions in life and, ultimately, our lives would be easier if our girls made good decisions. This conclusion was so self-evident it always made us laugh.

On February 14, 2001, Thoratec completed its merger with Thermocardio Systems. When Tom arrived home that night, it was the first time since we had been married he didn't bring me roses for Valentine's Day. "I worked so late that by the time I got to the store to get the roses, they were all sold out," he said. "I really didn't think you wanted them bad enough for me to go around to lots of different stores." I just laughed. We toasted each other and the completion of the merger with the bottle of champagne he had brought. Later when I remembered the flowers I didn't get, I realized it was the beginning of a year with a lot of firsts for us.

Even though Tom disliked giving gifts on what he considered arbitrary "obligation" days such as Christmas and birthdays, Tom surprised me with a birthday gift on March 10th: concert tickets to see Wynona and Naomi Judd. This was an amazing gift to me from Tom. I liked country music and he liked progressive. Just for him to sit through a Judd's concert was a stretch. I looked at him curiously, and he just replied, "I knew how much you'd enjoy going."

On the morning of April 12, Tom left for work and I noticed Madison was sleeping later than normal. Seven o'clock. Seven-thirty. She still wasn't coming downstairs. Halley came to me and reported that Madison was indeed awake but wouldn't talk to her. I immediately went upstairs to check and found Madison lying in bed, facing away from the door and not moving. I could hear her breathing slowly. Indeed her eyes were open. But she was staring blankly at the wall and drool was coming out of her mouth. I spoke her name. She didn't respond. When I touched her, her arm fell limp to one side. I knew she had suffered some kind of seizure. I yelled for Halley to bring the phone. I called Tom. "Come home. Something is wrong with Madison."

I called 911. At the emergency room, the doctors confirmed Madison had suffered a seizure. They believed she still was seizing so they cut off her pajamas and went to work. On one side of the table they kept pumping Phenobarbital into her; on the other side a doctor began giving her a spinal tap. Two people in the San Francisco Bay Area had recently died of spinal meningitis.

No matter what they tried, Madison wasn't responding. They couldn't get any movement out of her. Meanwhile she was lying on the table naked. Cool air was rushing in from the outside door. She was shivering. The nurses kept saying she was seizing but Tom and I insisted she was simply cold. "Close the door and cover her up," Tom said. Finally one of the nurses agreed. By this time she had received three adult-sized doses of Phenobarbital. As soon as the warm blanket covered her, she stopped shivering.

While the nurses performed more tests, one of the doctors said, "I'm going to go to CT with her in the event we have an expiration." I looked at Tom. Did the doctor think we didn't know the meaning of that word?

We had just gotten over thinking Halley was going to die. Now we were reliving a similar experience with another of our girls. Emotionally strained, we were able to remain remarkably calm. This was characteristic of the strong connection between Tom and myself. No matter what was going on in our lives, we had always been able to manage ourselves calmly during the most trying circumstances. It was a result of the deep trust and bond of love between us. In these and our faith in God we found our strength.

Tom and I spent the next four days in the hospital with Madison. For the first 24 hours she remained paralyzed, unable to speak or move. Slowly her speech returned, but she still couldn't walk on her own. But then to everyone's surprise, including the doctors, within one week, she made a full recovery.

Follow-up appointments to find out why she had suffered the seizure proved futile. The doctors said anyone could have one unexplained seizure in a lifetime and this was Madison's. The doctors also couldn't offer any explanation for her amazing recovery. We, on the other hand, believed her recovery was divine intervention. During her hospital stay, Madison had been covered in prayer by a multitude of prayer chains. We knew we had witnessed the power of prayer now not just once, but twice.

What we believed true for Madison we also believed true for Halley. There was little explanation for their recoveries. Not only did they improve, but their recoveries were complete.

I wondered if perhaps our faith was being tested. Was God checking to see if we would turn toward or away from Him when it seemed our child was dying? We knew that for us, there was only one choice. No matter what happened we would turn towards God because we knew only through our faith in His benevolent omnipotence could we find the peace, strength, and comfort to persevere through whatever we were facing.

Calm Before the Storm

Summer 2001 was the most relaxing we had had in years. We spent a lovely time together as a family: weekends at the park; trips to Lake Tahoe. We decided to spend Christmas vacation within driving distance of our home and had fun during the summer scouting out possible destinations.

The 4th of July we went to the beach with friends. This was another first. I was always the one who wanted to celebrate the 4th of July at the beach. Tom preferred to stay home. He didn't like crowded places and the beach was literally swarming on holidays. For whatever reason, he conceded this time. We had a great time, picnicking and playing Frisbee and football. For me, to smell the barbeque, see the families together, and have flags flying near their beach blankets, it felt like a perfect American holiday.

Later in July, the girls and I went to Arkansas to see my family while Tom went to our farm in Wisconsin. This was the first time Tom and I had had separate vacations since we were married. I wanted to see my family, but the farmhouse was also in need of repairs. We knew the girls and I would be in Tom's way in Wisconsin, so it only made sense to go separate ways.

The girls and I stayed in Arkansas for almost two weeks. Even though we had a nice time, when we returned home, I made a decision never to go on vacation without Tom again. Traveling for business was one thing, but choosing to be away from him when we could be together was another. Never again.

Tom traveled almost all of August. He was gone every weekend except one. The weekend he was home, we went camping at Mt. Shasta in northern California. Tom had wanted to scout out the area as another potential Christmas destination, since we had ruled out Lake Tahoe as too crowded and expensive. As always, Tom was going to make an informed decision. He prepared for the Mt. Shasta camping trip by purchasing books and studying campgrounds.

My mom, who had recently moved to California to be closer to us, joined us for one night of the campout. This surprised me because Mom was always so prim and proper. She always wore her makeup and jewelry, smelled of perfume, and combed her hair to perfection. Camping didn't seem to lend itself to the way she liked to be.

Through his reading Tom had learned that bears frequently roamed the Mt. Shasta camping area. Tom was adamant that my mother understand that a sweet scent of any kind might attract bears. Before settling down for the night, Mom asked Tom, "Would it be okay if I used lip balm?"

"Sure, it's okay," he replied. "It's just fine. You'll be in your tent and we'll be in ours."

Mom decided against the lip balm. We couldn't help but laugh.

In the middle of the night, Mom decided to go to her car and look for an extra blanket. Instead of using a flashlight, she turned on a lantern which lit up the campground for fifty yards in every direction.

Tom looked out through the screen of our tent and began giving the play-by-play in his best "Bill Murray" voice. "She's coming out of her tent. She's going to her car. She's opening the door. What is she doing?" I laughed uncontrollably. Since our second date I had always loved how Tom's spontaneous and unexpected antics could make me laugh.

It was such a fun trip. It was the last weekend Tom and I had together.

Chapter Five

The Last Day and the First

*"Death and sorrow will be the companions of our journey;
hardship our garment; constancy and valor our only shield.
We must be united, we must be undaunted, we must be inflexible."*
– Winston Churchill, October 8, 1940

We must never forget what happened to this country on September 11, 2001. I say this not out of any personal bias because Tom died, but because it reminds us that there is a price to achieve and maintain freedom. There always has been. Our freedom is always assailable. We must be willing to stand firm, stand up, and even fight for it when the need arises. We must be willing to do the right thing in the face of danger. We must be willing to lay down our lives, if called, to secure the future of our country for the generations who will follow us.

If we forget the horror of the events of 9/11, we can be tempted to fall into the complacency of thinking that if we don't pay attention to the conflicts in other countries that they won't pay attention to us. That day showed us that such a way of thinking is both naïve and dangerous.

And so, I will share my story from that day – Tom's last. I only can share it from my intensely personal perspective. You have your own story of how September 11th and the days and weeks which followed effected you. I encourage you to remember it. Remember how you were thinking. Remember how horrendous these attacks were. Remember how instead of fighting soldier to soldier, this enemy used innocent civilians as weapons to kill other innocent civilians. We must also remember to not stay stuck in the past, so we can move forward in the right way.

The Stage Is Set

Looking back it is easy to see how everything Tom and I had experienced in our lives up until that day was preparing us for what was to come. At the time though, we had no inkling of the magnitude of change the events of one day could bring to five ordinary lives.

The morning of Friday, September 7, I finally found a house that seemed just perfect for us. For almost a year we had been looking for a new home. We wanted a larger yard for the children, Tom needed an extra room for his office, and I wanted our three girls to have separate bedrooms as they grew older. It was the right price, the right number of rooms, and the right location.

Tom had flown out the previous Sunday afternoon for a short business trip to New York, returned on Tuesday, September 4, and left again the next day for the Pacific Northwest, then on to Southern California. I expected him home that afternoon for a few hours, but then he had to leave again Friday night for a quick visit to his family in Minnesota and then New York again.

The San Francisco Bay Area housing market still was turning around quickly, so I called his cell phone and asked Tom to make every effort he could to be home in time to go look at the house that afternoon. If we waited until after the weekend, I was certain the house would be sold. In true Tom Burnett style he promised to make it. He flew in at three o'clock and called me on his cell phone. He had a five o'clock meeting at the office, but would meet me with the realtor at six. The realtor had another meeting scheduled at six-thirty so it would be tight, but doable.

Tom didn't show up until 10 minutes before the realtor's next appointment. When he walked up Halley, Madison, and Anna Clare engulfed him. "Daddy, Daddy, Daddy!" they yelled. "Come look at the yard. Come look at the tree house." They took his hands and dragged him to the backyard. After a few minutes, I got his attention and pulled him into the house. As we looked around, he noticed a button on the wall. "Oh, what's this for?" he asked as he pushed it.

A five-alarm fire bell sounded. The kids screamed, and the realtor became irritated as she scrambled to try and figure out how to turn it off. The alarms continued to blare. Tom looked at me, laughing. "Why would they have a button there?"

Dumbstruck, I asked, "Why would you push a button in someone else's house?" He just made one of his goofy faces that always made me laugh.

The kids' screaming turned into crying because the noise was piercing. None of us could stand to be in the house another minute. We rushed outside and turned towards home.

When we arrived Tom caught me off guard. "What's for dinner?" he asked. When I explained I hadn't had time to prepare dinner because I'd been busy looking at houses all day, he seemed a little irritated. This was unlike him. Never, not once in our marriage had he expected me to cook dinner, even though I always did. In fact, I would cook such large dinners that just two months prior Tom had asked me not to cook for him at all anymore, but only for the children. "When I come in," he said, "I'll just have something light and I'll fix it myself." He had wanted to lose 10 pounds and the meals I cooked were anything but light.

That night we had leftovers. After dinner, we went upstairs to unpack his suitcases so we could pack them again. We talked about usual things in preparation for his flight out later that night: what we would be doing the following week; how the kids were doing in school. Anna Clare would begin pre-school on Tuesday, the 11th, and her sisters had just finished their first week of kindergarten. Tom asked about their teachers. His questions were atypically punctuated and short.

He was becoming more irritable by the minute, and I still didn't know why. Then what he'd bottled up all afternoon burst out of him. "You know what? I just hated that house today. Why did you have me go see that house? I busted my butt all day long to get here, and you had that house to show to me. Didn't you know I would hate that house?"

"No," I said, and for the second time that day I looked at him in disbelief. "I thought you would like it as much as I did."

The heated conversation then changed from what we wanted in a new house to him exploding about work, a subject he never talked about. While we were packing, he kept interjecting about how he didn't want to go on this trip. He was tired from all the travel and his workload was getting heavier and heavier with no end in sight. He was overloaded with just the volume of reports he had to go over. He needed to hire more people to ease the workload. And his travel schedule was only going to get worse. Over the next six weeks, he had meetings in cities across Europe and Asia. This weekend was just the beginning.

So that's why he was so irritable, I thought. He's overtired. Tom needed rest and some time alone. Even though the kids wanted to play with him, I sent them to bed early. Tom went downstairs and sat in front of the television, flipping through the channels while I stayed upstairs and finished unpacking and repacking his suitcases. When I was done, I went down to sit with him. He was watching a program about how to fly a commercial airplane, a program he'd already seen three or four times, feeding his insatiable hunger to learn again. We sat together in comfortable silence for about 20 minutes until yawning got the best of me. I tried to stay up because I wanted time with him, but by nine o'clock, he said reassuringly, "Go ahead and go to bed. I know you're tired. I'll wake you before I leave."

As I walked upstairs, I felt the familiar fear well up inside me, *What if he doesn't come home this time?* I turned around to start back down the stairs, but then stopped again. I was just so tired. *Oh, he always comes home. We'll sort this out on Tuesday when he gets back.* I went upstairs and fell asleep.

An hour and a half later Tom was standing at the end of our bed. He touched my foot to wake me up. "I'm getting ready to leave now."

"OK, I'll come down and lock the door," I said. The car service was waiting outside. "Tom, are you still angry?" I asked.

"No, I don't want you to think I'm angry at you. I'm not. It's just been a really tough week, a really bad week."

"I know."

We hugged goodbye on the doorstep and as he walked away I said, "I hope you have a good trip. Be safe." I always said that to him before he went away on a business trip. Always. "Be safe." And never once in the 10 years we were married had he responded. This time he turned around and looked me straight in the eyes and said, "You bet I will."

A chill came over me.

I watched as the driver opened the door. Tom climbed in and rode away.

It was Friday, September 7 at 10:30 p.m. That was the last time I saw my husband.

Tom's first stop before New York was Bloomington, Minnesota, so that he could spend the weekend with his parents. He also wanted to check on our farmhouse. The annual Thanksgiving deer hunt was approaching and his deer stand needed to be moved. On Saturday evening I spoke to Tom briefly, mostly about his day at the farmhouse. He had thought about staying there that night, but had decided to spend the time with his parents instead. Being back at the house he grew up in must have raised his spirits. He seemed relaxed and happy.

He called again late Sunday afternoon from the Minneapolis/St. Paul airport. He had spent a good portion of the day searching for his cell phone. He had made the rounds at a handful of sports equipment stores in town, looking for a new rifle, when he suddenly realized that he didn't have his phone anymore. He backtracked, returning to each of the stores in turn, calling his number using his mom's cell. But since his voice mail was full, his phone would only ring once. The chances were slim he would find it. At the fifth and last store, he heard the ring come from under a pile of sleeping bags. How it got there was anyone's guess. He was so thankful to have found it.

He apologized for being angry on Friday. "I want to go see that house again," he said.

"Yeah?"

"Yeah. Let's go ahead and look at it again on Tuesday when I get back. I wasn't in the right state of mind to go house hunting that afternoon. And if you really love it that much, on Wednesday we'll make an offer. But it's going to be a low-ball offer."

We laughed, since we both knew what that meant. We'd made many low-ball offers before, but since everything in California's real estate market was selling at a premium, offering something below the asking price was just silly.

On Monday morning I called his cell phone and caught him in the middle of a meeting, so I quickly told him what was going on at home. My 10-year-old Volvo had broken down at my mom's house and would have to be towed 45 miles for repair. I had checked prices and it was going to be expensive, so I wanted to hear what he thought about it before making the decision.

"I've got to get you a new car," was his first response. "The guy at the Ford dealership e-mailed me this morning. He said he would drop the price on that Expedition I test-drove." Then he said, "Don't do anything. Just leave the car where it is, and I'll take care of it when I get home." He said he would call later.

Tom and I spoke usually by phone several times every day, whether he was traveling or not. However, we ended up not connecting that night. When he called the children and I were having dinner at a friend's house. Though he normally would have called my cell phone if he couldn't reach me at home, for some reason he left a message instead. He wanted us to know he was thinking of us, that he hoped we had a good day, and he would see us tomorrow.

September 11, 2001

On Tuesday, September 11, the girls piled into our bedroom and woke me up before my alarm had the chance to go off at six o'clock.

Halley, Madison, and Anna Clare were excited. It was Anna Clare's first day of preschool, and they were being playful in a way I loved.

I didn't want to be late. I scurried the children downstairs, put on my slippers, and threw on Tom's blue robe, which I always wore when he traveled.

In the kitchen I started to cook breakfast and turned on the television. Our downstairs was one large open area, so it was easy to see the TV from any part of the kitchen/living area. As I removed the first waffles from the toaster, I looked up and saw footage of an airplane crashing into the World Trade Center. I turned up the volume to hear what had happened.

The girls were sitting around the breakfast table and became interested in what was going on, too. Like most people, my first thought was that there had been an air traffic control problem or that a private plane had struck the building by mistake. I didn't think much of it other than it seemed a somewhat surreal and odd accident. I continued making cinnamon waffles for the girls.

The reporters were asking eye witnesses what type of plane had crashed. They speculated it might be a prop plane, a cargo plane, or even a private plane. I kept watching the smoke coming out of the World Trade Center. As I stared at the television, it showed a second plane fly into the other tower. I couldn't believe it. What was going on?

Then I remembered Tom. What hotel was he staying in anyway? Was he at the Marriot in Times Square this time? How far was Times Square from the World Trade Center? I couldn't remember. I hadn't been to New York since my flight attendant days just before the girls were born. I did remember that representatives of Thoratec were opening the NASDAQ that morning. But where did that put Tom? Could he be walking around there somewhere where glass and debris might hit him?

The phone rang. It was Mom calling to ask if I was watching the morning news.

"Yes."

Then because her love often expressed itself in practical worry, she rattled off a series of questions. Do you know where Tom is? What time is he leaving New York? What airplane is he on? What is his flight number?

I told her all I knew. He was in New York somewhere and was supposed to come home later that morning. Mom said the plane which hit the World Trade Center was an American Airlines plane. "Well, don't worry, Mom, I know that Tom wouldn't be on an American Airlines plane."

"How can you be so sure?"

"He only flies United or Delta. Mom, the likelihood of that being Tom's plane is just minute. It just can't be his plane. Like I said, he'd be on United, so don't worry."

She said, "Okay," and hung up. I continued cooking breakfast, but with a watchful eye on the television. It was 6:10 a.m.

The newscasters were now reporting that both planes were indeed commercial airliners. This alarmed me even more and I tried to remember if Tom had left an itinerary, but he hadn't. All I could remember was what he had told me during one of our brief chats. If he finished his business early, then he would take an earlier flight and be home by noon. I started calculating how many hours the flight would take, accounting for the time changes, and realized this would mean he would have had to depart early in the morning.

I continued making waffles. My worry increased. I decided to try Tom's cell phone, but he didn't answer. This was not cause for immediate concern, because if he was on a flight already, use of cell phones was forbidden. I thought of calling his secretary, but it was so early she would still be in bed. I thought about calling Tom's mom, but didn't want to alarm her in case it was nothing.

As I tried to go about my business in the kitchen, undecided about who to call, the phone rang. It was Tom's mother who I called Mrs. Bev. (I had been taught as a child never to call an older adult by their first name out of respect, so even with Tom's parents, I referred to them as Mr. Tom and Mrs. Bev). She asked the same questions as my mother. Had I talked to Tom? No. Did I know what flight he was on? No. What time was his flight supposed to leave? I didn't know.

We talked about the airplane crashes in general while I served the girls their waffles. We still thought it was a major problem with air traffic control on the East Coast. She told me she'd spoken with Tom the night before at his hotel in Times Square, but this morning, when she tried to call his cell phone, there was no answer. Mrs. Bev asked me to please let her know if he called. I said I would, and was about to hang up when I heard my call waiting beep in. "Let me click over," I said. "It may be Tom."

"Okay. Call me back if it is."

I looked at the caller ID and indeed it was Tom's cell phone number. The time was 6:27 a.m.

"Hello?" I said.

"Deena."

"Tom, are you okay?" I asked.

"No, I'm not. I'm on an airplane that's been hijacked."

"Hijacked? Wow, you really are having a bad week."

"Can you believe this?"

Tom was speaking with concern – quickly and quietly – and yet with great authority. I thought I heard the hum of an airplane in the background.

"They just knifed a guy."

"A passenger?"

"Yes."

"Where are you? Are you in the air?" I didn't understand how he could be calling me on his cell phone from the air.

"Yes, yes, just listen. Our airplane has been hijacked. It's United Flight 93 from Newark to San Francisco. We are in the air. The hijackers have already knifed a guy. One of them has a gun. They're telling us there's a bomb on board. Please call the authorities. I'll hold on while you call."

"Tom, how can I call if you are on the line?"

"Get your cell phone."

"It's not charged up. I don't even know where it is!"

"Okay, I'll call you back." He hung up.

I had written down everything.

The entire call lasted only seconds. I had the feeling he was being watched; that he was hunched down behind a seat trying to keep from being noticed. I didn't want to lengthen the conversation and cause him any trouble. Because of my flight attendant training I knew I shouldn't draw attention to him if there was a crisis during the flight, and I was very afraid for him for making that call.

I became very still. It seemed like my whole body just stopped. I couldn't move. I could feel myself not breathing. *You have to take a breath, Deena. Take a breath.*

Then I realized my children were huddled around me. They knew it had been their dad on the phone. During the call, they had been reaching for the receiver, asking if they could talk to him. "Daddy can't talk to you right now," I explained. "He's having a little problem on the airplane. He'll talk to you later."

They said okay and went back to watching re-running footage of the airplane flying into the World Trade Center on television. With them occupied, I took my first step. When I did, I felt a jolt of energy from absolute terror surge through my body. I didn't know where to direct the energy, what to do, what to look for, who to call, or even what to say if I got someone on the telephone. High pressure situations were easy for Tom. Not so much so for me.

I started sifting through loose papers on the kitchen counter, looking for something but not knowing what I was looking for. I was frantic. Who do I call? Who do I call? I reached into the cabinet and pulled out the telephone book. I started flipping through the blue pages – the Federal Government listings. Nothing seemed helpful *OK. 911. I have to call 911. Maybe they can help.*

I dialed 911. *The person on the other end is going to think I am insane.*

It was 6:31 a.m. A woman answered. As deliberately and slowly as I could muster I said, "My name is Deena Burnett." I specifically told the operator my name so she would know I wasn't some crazy person making a prank phone call. "My husband is on an airplane that has been hijacked. He just called me from the airplane on his cellular telephone. He told me they have a bomb on board." Then I gave her the flight number and the route.

"Your husband is on a hijacked airplane?" she asked.

"Yes." She questioned everything I said, to clarify and confirm it. I don't imagine she had received many phone calls like mine, but she was very calm and collected. I was relieved that I didn't feel like I had to convince her I was telling the truth.

"Hold on just a moment and let me switch you to the police department."

A man answered. I explained to him what was going on. He asked me to hold and switched me to the FBI. Eventually, I ended up speaking with a special agent. Getting to the right person took about two minutes. "Are you talking about the planes that just hit the World Trade Center?" he asked.

"No. I know about those two planes. This is another plane."

"A third plane?!"

"Yes. This is a third plane."

I had to convince him I had actually spoken to my husband after the two other planes had crashed. Precious minutes were ticking by. I was getting frustrated. This was absolutely useless. What could they do? They were here on the ground and Tom was six miles in the air, thousands of miles away. *But this is all I can do.*

Once the special agent finally believed me, he started going over questions he wanted me to ask Tom if I spoke to him again. How many hijackers were on board? What kind of weapons did they have?

Suddenly I couldn't find the paper and pen I had when I was talking to Tom, so I started looking for them to write the agent's questions down. Simultaneously I was walking up and down the stairs, trying to get the girls ready for school. Call waiting beeped again. Tom was back. It was 6:34 a.m.

"Hello?" I said.

"They're in the cockpit. The guy they knifed is dead."

"He's dead?"

"Yes. I tried to help him, but I couldn't get a pulse."

"Tom, they are hijacking planes all up and down the East coast," I told him. "They are taking them and hitting designated targets. They've already hit both towers of the World Trade Center." He became quiet. I thought we had lost the connection.

Then he said, "They're talking about crashing this plane." He paused. "Oh my gosh! It's a suicide mission."

I kept quiet as I heard him repeat to others what I said. I could hear people talking in the background, as if the information was being passed around, but I couldn't understand what anyone was saying.

"Who are you talking to?" I asked.

"My seatmate. Do you know which airline is involved?"

"No. They don't know if they're commercial airlines or not. The news reporters are speculating it could be cargo planes, private planes, or commercial airliners. No one knows."

"How many planes are there?"

"They're not sure. At least three. Maybe more."

"Okay, okay. Do they know who is involved?"

"No."

Then Tom said, "We're turning back toward New York. We're going back to the World Trade Center. No, wait, we're turning back the other way. We're going south."

"What do you see?" I asked.

"Just a minute, I'm looking. I don't see anything. We're over a rural area. It's just fields. I've gotta go." He hung up.

The second call lasted about two minutes. I called Martha, Tom's older sister, and told her to get over to her parents' house because I was about to call them and they were going to need her. She asked if Tom was okay. I said I didn't know and told her about his flight and the phone calls. She said she was on her way.

I called the Burnett's. Martha walked through the door while I was talking. I knew they would be fine as long as she was there.

After I hung up, I slumped down in Tom's recliner rocking chair. The children were sitting on the sofa next to me as I held the phone. It rang again. It was Tom's younger sister, calling from her cell phone on her way to work.

"Deena, its Mary Margaret. Have you heard from Tom?"

"Yes. He's on a plane that has been hijacked. He just called me from the air. I just spoke with your parents and Martha is with them. I can't talk."

"Okay, I'm turning around and going there also. Call me later."

I said I would and hung up. I was watching the TV as a headline flashed on the screen that another plane had crashed into the Pentagon. They weren't saying the flight number or giving any other details. I immediately thought it was Flight 93. I just knew it.

Then I started wailing, making sounds like a dying animal. I couldn't believe such sounds were coming out of me. At first the children thought I was playing a game and started laughing. Then they saw the tears. All three girls ran over and climbed into my lap. They started crying and wanted to know what was wrong.

I've got to stop crying. I'm upsetting the children. Why can't I stop?

I kept trying to stop, but couldn't. I kept looking at the clock. *He hasn't called back! He hasn't called back!*

Then the phone rang. My first thought was that he had survived the plane crash. I immediately pulled myself together and answered the phone. It was Tom. It was 6:45 a.m.

"Deena."

"Tom, you're okay?" I said.

"No, I'm not."

"They just hit the Pentagon."

Then I heard him repeat those exact words to the people around him.

"Okay, okay. What else can you tell me?"

"They think five airplanes have been hijacked. One is still on the ground. They believe all of them are commercial planes. I haven't heard them say which airline, but all of them have originated on the East Coast."

"Do you know who is involved?" he asked.

"No."

"What is the probability of them having a bomb on board?" Pause. "I don't think they have one," he said, answering his own question. "I think they're just telling us that for crowd control."

My flight attendant training kicked in. "A plane can survive a bomb if it's in the right place," I said.

"Did you call the authorities?"

"Yes, they didn't know anything about your plane."

"They're talking about crashing this plane into the ground. We have to do something. I'm putting a plan together."

"Who's helping you?"

"Different people. Several people. There's a group of us. Don't worry. I'll call you back."

He could tell that I was concerned, and yet it was as if he was at Thoratec, sitting at his desk, and we were having a regular conversation. It was the strangest thing because he was using the same tone of voice I had heard a thousand times. It calmed me to know he was so confident. I felt like everything was going to be okay.

The doorbell rang. When I went to the door, I saw a huge policeman in a dark blue suit with a badge. Startled, I screamed in fear. I don't know why his appearance made me so afraid, but it did. Then I flung the door wide open, turned, and walked back toward the TV. The officer followed me in. I was rushing around the house, still trying to get the girls ready for school, when Tom called back a fourth time. It was 6:54 a.m.

"Tom?"

"Hi. Anything new?" he asked.

"No."

"Where are the kids?"

"They're fine. They're sitting at the table having breakfast. They're asking to talk to you."

"Tell them I'll talk to them later."

"I called your parents. They know your plane has been hijacked."

"Oh…you shouldn't have worried them. How are they doing?"

"They're okay. Mary and Martha are with them."

"Good." Long pause. "We're waiting until we're over a rural area. We're going to take back the airplane."

"No! Sit down. Be still. Be quiet. Don't draw attention to yourself."

"Deena! If they're going to crash this plane into the ground, we're going to have to do something."

"What about the authorities?" I pleaded.

"We can't wait for the authorities. I don't know what they could do anyway. It's up to us. I think we can do it."

"What do you want me to do?"

"Pray, Deena. Just pray."

"I am!"

"Don't worry. I'll be home for dinner. I may be late, but I'll be home."

"Okay."

There was a long pause.

"I love you," I said.

"Don't worry, Deena," he said. "We're going to do something." Then he hung up.

It wasn't a hurried conversation. In fact, there were seconds where we sat quietly on the phone. Like so many other conversations in our marriage, he felt comfortable that I was on the other end, and I felt the same way. The whole call lasted less than two minutes.

I didn't doubt Tom was capable of handling the situation on the plane. His parents used to say there was nothing their Tommy couldn't do and I believed it. Throughout our conversation Tom had remained calm and collected. He was doing what he always did, collecting information, analyzing it, devising a plan, and moving forward to execute it.

However, there was a moment during that long pause in the middle of our conversation when for the first time I thought I might not get to talk to him again. For this reason I needed him to hear I loved him.

Even though I had written down every question the FBI wanted me to ask, I couldn't ask them. I didn't want to take up any precious time talking any more than was necessary. I had wanted to hear Tom's voice. Instead, I wrote down everything he said and everything that was going on.

It didn't bother me that he didn't say, "I love you" in return. Tom wasn't thinking these would be his last words to me. He honestly expected to be home later that morning. If he thought he was going to die on that plane, he would have called his parents and sisters and talked to his daughters. At the very least, he would have given me a message for them. But he didn't ask to speak to any of them. He was fighting to live.

Anyway, if Tom really had thought this would be the last time we'd speak, his last words would have been something of more significance than "I love you." I already knew that he loved me. He didn't have to tell me that. He would have said something about raising his children. It would have been something about living a godly life. He even might have joked about getting to heaven and finally knowing the answers to all life's mysteries. It would have been very typical of Tom to use humor in such a situation. He would have been concerned for me and have wanted to allay my fears.

Within minutes of the fourth call, the FBI agent I had spoken to earlier called back. "Have you heard from Tom again?" he asked.

"I just got off the phone with him."

He seemed surprised. "Did he say anything about the hijackers, like how many there were? Or did he describe them? Did he say what language they were speaking?"

"No, no, no."

"Okay, did you hear anything in the background?"

"Just other people speaking English. They seemed to be sitting near my husband. Tom was relaying information to them as I provided it from the TV. During the fourth call, the background was silent."

He started asking more questions, when I interrupted and asked, "Have you tried to call Tom's cell phone?"

"We tried, but there was no answer." Pause. "Mrs. Burnett, would it be all right if we sent some people over to your house to talk to you?"

"Sure."

The conversation was brief. Neither of us wanted to tie up the phone line. It wouldn't take them long to get here. After I hung up, the policeman asked me why I hadn't tried to call Tom. I said that Tom had been calling me regularly, every five to 10 minutes. I had no reason to think he wouldn't continue. What I didn't say was that I was afraid to call him. I didn't want to draw any unnecessary attention to him.

My neighbor Dena walked in. She began asking about the children, wondering if one of them was sick. I told her no. I explained that Tom was on a plane that had been hijacked. That he was putting together a plan to take back the plane. "Sounds just like something Tom would do," she said. "My husband wouldn't sit still either."

For a moment we even giggled about the situation. I was so sure Tom was going to be okay. It never dawned on me there could be circumstances beyond his control. After Dena left, I told the children to go upstairs and brush their teeth. Then I called two friends, Debbie and Gina, and explained what was going on. I asked them to pick up the kids and take them to school. They understood why I didn't want to leave the house.

By 7:30 a.m., it had been 36 minutes since Tom called. All four of his other calls had come at close intervals. I was watching the television and keeping my eye on the clock, aware of each individual minute as it ticked by.

I wasn't too worried yet. He didn't have time to call back. He was busy saving the plane.

Firemen, policemen, and paramedics continued to arrive. One of them asked to take my blood pressure. "Why? No. No. I don't need you to check my blood pressure," I exclaimed, not understanding why they were there. I continued to stay in motion, moving about the house. One of the policemen was playing with the girls inside. Then they went outside to see the fire trucks and police cars. Tom's assistant, Kim, at Thoratec called. "Have you spoken to Tom?" she asked.

"Yes, but..."

"Oh good, then he's okay. We have so many people in New York right now, we're just trying to locate everyone."

"No, he's not okay. He's on an airplane that's been hijacked. It's United Airlines Flight 93 from Newark to San Francisco."

"It's been hijacked?"

"Yes, he's been calling me from the plane, but he hasn't called in a while. There's a policemen here, so I'll let you talk to him."

A new policeman came on duty. The phone was ringing non-stop. Call-waiting was beeping in so often it was virtually impossible to carry on a conversation. My step-mom called while she was on her way to work, wanting to know if Tom was traveling that morning. I told her about the plane. "Oh Deena. Oh, no!" She began to cry. I told her I would call her back.

By eight o'clock, I realized it had been over an hour since I last spoke with Tom. My anxiety level was rising. Inside I was beginning to be afraid of what had been happening on that plane. Maybe I didn't have to worry. Maybe he had landed the plane successfully and just hadn't been able to call yet. But it had been over an hour...

Debbie and Gina arrived simultaneously to pick up the girls for school. The policemen helped move car seats from vehicle to vehicle. As I got the kids ready, making sure they were buckled in with backpacks and everything they needed, I acted as if it were a normal day with hugs and kisses. I told the girls I would see them later on, and wished Anna Clare a fun day at pre-school. Walking back into the house, I realized the phone was still clenched in my hand.

Each time it rang I jumped, even though I was trying to act calm.

I thought about the children. At least they were happy to be going to school. They were having an exciting morning, seeing fire trucks and police cars up close for the first time. They had sensed something wrong earlier. They saw the footage of the airplane crash into the World Trade Center tower and kept asking if it was daddy's plane. I reminded them I had just spoken to their father and he said he would be home later that day. They could talk to him then. Every time the phone rang, they asked if that was him. They always talked to him when he called, and when I wouldn't let them, they knew something was going on.

Shortly after the girls left, the fire trucks left, too. It was just the one policeman, named Chris Stangle and me. We started going over the same questions the other policeman had asked. His walkie-talkie was going off constantly. He tried to get me to eat something, but I wasn't hungry. I was glued to the television. I thought about switching the channel, thinking that another station might provide better coverage, but I was afraid that during the second it took to change the channel, I might miss something. I felt increasingly frustrated. The news reports weren't providing any updates – no names of the airlines, no flight numbers. Nothing.

Then I remembered the FBI was on their way. I needed to dress. I was still wearing Tom's blue robe and my slippers. I told the policeman I was going upstairs to shower. "Okay, but leave the telephone with me," he said.

"No. Absolutely not. You're not talking to my husband. No one's talking to him. I'll take the phone so I won't miss a phone call."

"But Mrs. Burnett, you might not hear the phone in the shower."

"I can hear it just fine." I went upstairs.

The phone sat on the ledge adjacent to the shower facing me. It was the fastest shower of my life.

Still holding the phone, I got dressed, pulled my hair back, and went downstairs. Waiting at the bottom of the stairs stood Officer Stangle. I knew something was wrong. As soon as I got to the bottom, he said, "I think I have bad news for you."

I ran to the television. It was 9:00 a.m. and the reporter was talking about another flight that had just crashed. I turned to Officer Stangle and asked, "Is that Tom's flight?"

"Yes."

My knees buckled and I began to fall. My body felt like it weighed a thousand pounds. He caught me and guided me over to the couch. I sank into the sofa and sobbed. I buried my face into the couch because I didn't want this strange man watching me cry. It felt very odd to have a stranger sitting so close to me at such a horrible time. He didn't say anything. He just put his hand on my shoulder. I tried to sit up, but couldn't. I fell back against the cushions and cried more. He found tissue for me.

"Do you want me to turn the television off?" he asked.

"No," I could barely get out the word. He turned the volume down very low, though. I wept for quite a while. It was as if I was feeling every emotion I have ever felt all at once, caught up in sobbing and tears. A deeper-than-deep sadness consumed me, a hurt heavier than I had ever felt in my life. Nothing in my past ever prepared me for something like this. People close to me had died before, but this was a sorrow deeper than can even be put into words.

I cried, really sobbing, for about 20 minutes. The room was silent, except for the barely audible sounds coming from the television. The telephone was still clenched in my hand as if I were still expecting Tom to call.

"Officer, have they shown the crash site on TV?" I struggled to ask.

"No, they haven't." he said.

People can survive a plane crash. Then the phone rang and for a second I had hope that he was still alive.

"Deena? It's Martha. Have you heard from Tom?" she said.

"No," I screamed, sobbing. "He's dead!" As I sobbed and moaned into the phone, she kept saying, "Deena, I can't understand you. You have to calm down. You have to get hold of yourself. I can't understand what you're saying."

I screamed again, "He's dead! The plane crashed!"

"Do you know for sure that he's dead? Did United Airlines call and tell you there were no survivors?"

"No, no. I heard it on the television."

"We saw it, too. But have you talked to anyone at United?"

"No."

"Deena, I want you to know that the Lord is with you at all times."

Her remark angered me. "I don't need the Lord to be with me," I yelled back. "I needed Him to be with Tom."

"He is with Tom."

I couldn't talk to her anymore. Then I saw the crash site on TV and realized there could be no survivors. Stunned, I finally let go of the phone. Tom had been just 38 years old. He'd boarded Flight 93 in Newark in the hopes of getting home early, now he wasn't coming home at all – ever.

My world had turned upside down and would never be the same. Shortly thereafter the police chaplain came. He held my hands as we prayed.

"We never know why these things happen and there's no explanation. As long as you trust in God, He will bring you comfort," he said. He leaned forward to hug me and added, "There are wonderful organizations for widows."

Widow. Widow. Widow! Oh my goodness! I hadn't thought of that. My husband was in a plane crash. I hadn't quite thought of myself as a widow, but already I'm being labeled.

I lowered my head and began sobbing again.

The chaplain had meant well, but he couldn't find the words to make me feel better. Officer Stangle came over and led him outside. Then the policeman asked me, "Is there anyone from your church you might like to talk to?"

The only person who came to mind was Father Frank. Although our family was active at St. Isidore's, we didn't know the priests personally. It was a big parish. Three thousand members. Every service had a different priest.

Tom held great respect for Father Frank. Everything was black and white for him, and Tom was very much that way, too. Officer Stangle called over the scanner to have Father Frank summoned.

Walking to the bathroom in search of more tissue, I glanced into the living room and saw three men sitting quietly, making notes. *Where did they come from? I didn't hear anyone come in, and I certainly didn't hear anyone talking.*

One of them had his head down, and when I walked over, he looked up with a markedly sad countenance. In an effort to make him feel more comfortable, I said hello and kept walking. He gave a slight nod.

Then, tissue in hand, he rose and introduced himself. "Hello, Mrs. Burnett, we're with the FBI. When you get a chance, we'd like to talk with you."

"All right. Let's do it now." I said, leading them to the family room.

Like the police before him, he started asking a series of questions. He wanted to know what Tom said in the four phone calls. What did my husband do for a living? Why was Tom in New York? Where was he staying and how long was he there? Who was he seeing? Did he have any enemies, someone who might want to hurt him?

I became alarmed. Was he suggesting that my husband had something to do with this plane crash? That the plane crash might be his fault? That Tom might somehow be connected to the hijackers?

Maybe I shouldn't be answering their questions. Maybe I need an attorney. No, I know I haven't done anything wrong. Tom hasn't done anything wrong. Surely it can't hurt to just talk to them.

After 30 minutes or so of questioning, the agent seemed satisfied and went outside. Then the second agent began asking questions. The exact same ones. When he was finished, the third agent chimed in and started going over the same questions again.

Each time, they assured me that they didn't think I was lying. They just wanted to make sure I wasn't forgetting anything.

I couldn't focus on what they were saying. I couldn't even concentrate on what I was saying.

Then I remembered something about the third phone call. At one point, Tom asked me what I thought the probability was of there being a bomb on board. Before I could say anything, he answered his own question. "I don't think there's a bomb on board. I think they're just telling us that for crowd control."

After I shared that with the agent, I said, "I'm not sure why Tom asked me that."

"Well, maybe he was afraid," said the agent.

Still dazed, at first I found myself agreeing with him, but then I remembered how calm Tom had been. I looked at the agent squarely. "No, you didn't know my husband. He wasn't afraid."

The entire situation was surreal. My husband had just died on a hijacked plane. I had spoken to him minutes before his death. I knew that the plane crashing into the field was a direct result of his actions. Now I was talking to the FBI. There were police and firemen in my house. I felt like I was floating above the room, watching everything going on below.

This is not my life. My life is quiet, suburban, and ordinary. Things like this don't happen to people like us. We don't have policemen in our homes. We don't get questioned by the FBI. This is cannot be real.

I must have spent over an hour with them before they finished. One by one as they left, they gave me their business card with a number scratched on the back. Each told me the same thing, "Call if you think of anything else."

Suddenly I remembered I had taken notes. "I wrote it down. I have everything written down." I said. I ran to the kitchen counter and grabbed the day's errand list. Scratched all over the paper were notes from the conversations Tom and I had had. I looked at them carefully.

"Four times. He called four times."

The FBI reached for the paper, but I held it closer, refusing to let them have it.

"You wouldn't be able to read it anyway."

"Is there anything on there we should know that you haven't already told us?" the agent said.

"No."

"Okay. We'll check back with you later in the day."

As the FBI left, Father Frank entered. He was dressed traditionally in black with a white collar, except for the Birkenstock sandals he had on his feet. His eyes were blank as he walked towards me. It was obvious he did not know me.

Like the chaplain before him, he took my hand and sat next to me. "I know this has been a very bad morning for you. Why don't we start with a prayer?"

Father Frank prayed for peace and comfort in my life, the children's, and Tom's soul. He prayed for me to surrender to God's will and asked God to guide me in His path. He prayed for God to show me the way in raising my children and the way I should go in life.

While he prayed over me, I felt the presence of God wash into my spirit. I became calm. In the midst of all this chaos, I knew God was with me.

"All I want is to be in the presence of God," I said. "All I want is peace."

I knew I had to go to church as soon as I could.

We chatted briefly and I decided just to talk to him. I began to tell him about the cell phone conversations, about how Tom told me he had a plan and was going to do something. I told him they were going to try to take back the plane, which I knew Tom could have flown that airplane. But something must have gone wrong because I knew he could do it. He must not have had time to figure everything out. Maybe they were too low to the ground or maybe someone didn't follow one of his orders.

Anger began to build in me. There was Tom. He knew what he was doing. I knew he was in charge. I knew he could do anything. Maybe someone else's incompetence had caused the crash. Now he was dead. For what seemed like the first time in Tom's life, he had not succeeded.

This just couldn't be. Tom never failed at anything. *He* was the one on the phone telling me he had a plan. *He* was going to do something. I believed him. To find out that the plane crashed and that he wasn't coming home was unfathomable.

I was lost in my own thoughts, trying to put some sense of order to what had happened. Father Frank stood up. "Well Deena, I have to go. We have 20 other people in the parish who travel, and we want to make sure they're OK."

I wanted him to stay, but was afraid to ask for more time. It was hard to watch him leave.

As Father Frank walked out, Mom walked in. We gave each other a big hug.

"I got your message and knew immediately something was wrong. Has he called?" she asked.

"No. The plane crashed."

Mom started to cry, but gathered herself quickly. On her face was an expression I had seen many times throughout my childhood, in control, stoic. During difficult moments it was her habit to hold back her emotions and appear expressionless.

On the sofa, I began telling her what had happened.

She interrupted. "How much money do you have in the bank?"

Puzzled, I looked up at her.

"You'll need to call Social Security and talk to them about survivor benefits. You're definitely going to have to sell the house. Do you want to move back to Arkansas or move to Minnesota?"

My head began to spin. The reality of Tom's death was bearing down on me. *Oh my goodness! I can't afford this house. How am I going to make the house payment? We're going to have to move out.*

I lowered my head and began rubbing my temples.

She continued. "What are you going to do for work? You're going to have to go back to school and get your Masters. What are you going to get it in?"

My mom had always been practical, and I knew she was worried. Expressing her concern in this manner was her way of letting me know she loved me, but at that moment it was more than I could bear. My mind couldn't switch tracks that quickly. My husband had just died. There was nothing left in me left to process anything else.

Emotionally exhausted, I replied, "I can't think about this right now." I closed my eyes and put my hands to my head.

This was the third conversation I had had this morning with someone who I hoped would console me. It seemed that what I needed at that moment no one could give me. My pain was simply too great and my expectations too high of what someone outside myself could do to help. I started to cry. Normally I was the comforter, not the one who needed to be comforted. I couldn't believe what was happening. This just was not my life!

Officer Stangle came over, knelt down in front me, and took my hand. Then he looked at my Mom and said, "All of that can wait. She doesn't have to do anything right now."

Then he looked at me and said, "First of all, you're not going to have to sell this house and here's why. It sounds like your husband had a good job. I'm sure he has a financial plan in place to take care of you and the children. Because of the way he died, you're going to have enough people helping, that you will be able to stay in this house and raise your children the way you want to. You're not going to have to worry about any of that right now. And if none of that comes through, I am personally going to make sure you can stay in this house. If that's what you want. The police have wonderful resources. We can help you. You don't have to worry about anything."

Officer Stangle said the words I needed to hear. They brought a calm in the midst of a great, seemingly never-ending storm. Even though he had no way of knowing my financial circumstances, it didn't matter. I knew he was making guarantees he couldn't keep, but I didn't care. At that moment, his were the words I needed to hear.

My mom was right. I was going to have to think about these things. But Officer Stangle was right, too. I didn't have to do it immediately.

"Mom, I know you're right, but we're not going to do anything today. I don't want to talk about it anymore. I know these things have to be taken care of, but not today. Tomorrow. Okay?"

She agreed not to bring it up again.

I got up to turn off the television and noticed the front door was halfway open. Outside I saw dozens and dozens of people. Not only were there policemen and police cars, but also neighbors and friends from the school and church. They all wanted to see me, but the police wouldn't let anyone by. Bags full of groceries, flowers, and messages were beginning to pile up in the entryway.

The phone was ringing, but no one answered it. When the ringing stopped, I called United Airlines and asked about Flight 93. "Were there any survivors?"

They said they didn't know the plane had even crashed. They suggested I call back or they would contact me when they knew something.

Officer Stangle found me and said, "You've got some friends outside who really want to see you, and they say they aren't leaving until they do."

I went to the door and saw Michelle and Monica. They were both in their workout clothes. I was so happy to see their friendly, familiar faces.

As they came in, my mom went outside. The three of us sat down, and I told them everything. We cried together, hugged, and held hands. They asked if there was anything I needed. I said no. They asked if I had eaten anything. I said not yet, but I would later. After an hour, they left. They told me to call if I needed anything.

Around noon Debbie called to tell me she was going to pick up the kids after school and would take care of them until the evening. Once they got to her house, she called a few more times to let me know they were fine. "Deena, I haven't told them. I'm not letting them watch TV, so they have no idea," she said. "I'll bring the girls back around five o'clock."

I realized then that if I was going to go to church, I had to do it now. Officer Stangle was now off duty but said he would take me. "You're in no condition to be driving."

When we arrived at St. Isidore's, he stayed in his truck while I went in through a back door. I expected to be the only person there, but of course I wasn't. There were several people praying. I went to light a candle, but they had all been lit. Even the spares. At this point I had no idea how dramatically the events of that morning had impacted the entire country, let alone the world. I was completely enveloped in a grief which was excruciatingly personal.

I sat down and began praying for guidance. I tried not to cry, but couldn't help myself. I cried quietly, trying not to disturb anyone. But the harder I tried to keep quiet, the louder I sounded. I quickly went through all the tissue in my purse. The church was older with a high ceiling and stained glass windows. It was built with great acoustics for carrying choir music throughout. Today, it was my sobbing which echoed through the church. I wondered if anybody else here had known someone who died on September 11th.

As I sat there failing in my attempts not to be a disturbance, a woman sat down beside me. She handed me a box of tissue. She didn't say anything. Neither did she look at me. She bowed her head and began praying. I turned toward her. I tried to whisper, but through the sobbing the words came out too loudly. "My husband is dead. He was on one of the planes." The quiet of the church made it seem as though I was shouting.

She placed her hand on my back and bowed her head lower. I continued, "He was on one of the planes that crashed." I was embarrassed that everyone could hear. I tried to be more quiet.

She looked up at me and said, "I'm so sorry. I'm so very sorry." I was looking right at her and yet I couldn't see her face through the tears.

Crying, still crying, I couldn't believe I had so many tears inside of me. I was glad she was sitting there. I wondered if I knew her or if she knew me. To this day, I don't know who she was, but I will always remember the compassion that God enabled to flow from her to me. She served as the angel God knew I needed.

After a while, more people started coming in for a special service. The priest took the altar and said there was a member of the parish who had been killed that day. He did not mention Tom's name, only that we should pray for his soul and his family. People were looking around. I could tell they wanted to know who it was. It seemed as if everyone were looking at me.

After praying part of the rosary, I knew I needed to get home. It was late afternoon. The girls would be home soon.

On the way, Officer Stangle told me that he had called his wife and though off duty would like to stay with me and serve me as a personal bodyguard of sorts. In addition, he wanted me to know there had been news reporters at the church. They had intercepted the message sent over the police scanner earlier when the priest from St. Isidore's was requested. They had gone first to the police department, but the police wouldn't release Tom's name. Next they had gone to the church to ask who had been killed. Father Frank must have given Tom's name out.

At home, the FBI returned. They asked if I remembered anything else. We talked briefly, but I couldn't think of anything new. They told me specifically not to say anything to anyone about my cell phone conversations with Tom, especially the media because it was part of their investigation.

When they asked if there was anything they could do for me, I told them I wanted to hear the cockpit recordings. I wanted to know with more certainty what Tom went through during the last moments of his life. I needed to know what went wrong.

"I don't have the authority to release that information, but I'll pass along your request to those who do."

As the agents left, Debbie came in with the girls. It was almost suppertime.

The children were surprised the police were still here. The girls also asked about all the flowers and groceries. The refrigerators and cabinets were stocked, and the tables and counters had no more room. I decided it was best to send them upstairs to their playroom.

"Deena, I want you to know that the girls are doing just fine," said Debbie. "They're not aware of anything that's happened. Dan came home and my brother came over, and we played with them all afternoon."

But I could tell the girls knew something was not right. They had seen people still gathered on the street in front of our house. They knew the police were still here. At some point I was going to have to tell them about their father. I just didn't know when or how.

The girls came down for dinner. Debbie had brought pizza. While the girls ate, they talked about their day. Anna Clare was especially excited about her first day of pre-school. She showed me a teddy bear she had drawn and colored.

Officer Stangle told me that the press was beginning to arrive. He had been warning me all day that it was only a matter of time. He was right. They had Tom's name and we were listed in the phone book.

I became worried. *Oh no. What do they want? I can't talk to them. What am I going to say?*

News crews began filling the narrow subdivision street and spreading across the small lawns in our neighborhood. The phone continued ringing non-stop and so did the doorbell. They all wanted to talk to me, but I told Officer Stangle to tell them I had nothing to say. "You heard the FBI tell me not to talk to the media," I said.

Police were coming in and out, trying to keep the news reporters at bay. Meanwhile, more neighbors stopped by to see what was going on.

Several hours passed and Officer Stangle was becoming frustrated. "You know, you're going to have to talk to these people at some point," he said. "Do you want to go ahead and prepare a statement? I can read it or you can go out there and read it yourself. And then tell them that's all you have to say."

"What do you say in a statement?" I asked. "A statement about what? I have no idea what to talk about. They know who I am. They know who Tom is. They know how he died. What else am I going to tell them?"

"If you want, I'll have our public information officer prepare a statement on your behalf. He can read it."

"Okay, that's fine. You do it. You take care of it. I'm not saying anything to anyone. And I'm certainly not going out there."

I was afraid of them. I had seen too much television news over the years and didn't have enough broadcast experience to be clear on how to protect myself when I was the one being interviewed. I had never enjoyed public speaking of any sort, let alone on camera. I was a quiet housewife and I liked my life the way it was. Now there were news reporters and TV cameras at my front door. All I wanted was for them to go away, but they were doggedly persistent.

"All right, I'll take care of the press statement." Then he said, "When are you going to tell the children?"

"I'm not going to tell them until tomorrow."

"Why?"

"Because I want some time to think about what I'm going to say. I don't want to say something I'm going to regret. If I have to tell them tonight, I may do that."

"Well, you have a choice. Either you can tell them or they're going to find out from a news reporter. They can look outside the window themselves and see these people. I think it would be better coming from you than from someone else."

I knew he was right. Putting aside concerns about the media for the moment, I went upstairs and found the girls having fun in their toy room. Leading them down the hallway to their bedroom, I tried to get them to settle down and sit on their beds, but they wanted to play. They kept running back and forth to the window. The day had been exciting. Anna Clare kept asking, "Why are those people outside, Mommy? Why do they have cameras? Are they taking pictures of us?"

I was getting irritated. This wasn't how it was supposed to go. I was annoyed that I had to tell the children about Tom before I'd had time to collect my thoughts and plan what I wanted to say. In addition, I still couldn't get the girls to be still. All they wanted to do was play. Halley was sitting on the bed paging through a book while Madison and Anna Clare were running around the room with toys, occasionally stopping to look through the window blinds. I didn't know what else to do, so I just started talking.

"Girls, do you remember this morning when I told you Daddy was having a little problem on the airplane?"

Halley stopped and said, "Yes, I remember." Then she continued looking at her book.

"Well, Daddy did have a problem on the airplane, a very big problem. There were bad people on the airplane. And the bad people made the airplane crash. When the airplane crashed, everyone died. Including your father."

All three of them froze. They looked at me and were very still. Madison and Anna Clare climbed up on the bed next to me.

"Daddy died?" said Halley.

"No, no, no, no, no!" cried Madison.

Anna Clare put her head down on the bed and began to cry, too. Halley closed her book, climbed into my lap, and her tears flowed.

"Why did Daddy have to die?" asked Anna Clare.

"You know how we have talked about good people and bad people in the world?"

They all nodded.

"Well, there were some bad people on Daddy's airplane today. No one knew they were there until the airplane was in the air. They wanted to hurt the people on the airplane."

"Daddy tried to stop the bad people from hurting the good people. But the airplane crashed."

"Is Daddy an angel now?" asked Madison through her tears.

"Yes," I said softly.

"Where is he?" asked Halley.

"Well, Daddy's with Jesus in Heaven. That's where he lives now, and he can't come home."

"Why does Daddy want to be with Jesus instead of us?" asked Madison.

"Daddy didn't choose to live with Jesus. He wanted to be here with us. But we don't get to decide when to go to Heaven."

"Well, can we visit him?" asked Madison.

"No".

"Well, can I write him a letter?" asked Halley.

"No honey, we can't send him a letter."

"Can I call him on his cell phone?" asked Madison.

"No. They don't have cell phones in Heaven."

I needed to show that everything was going to be all right. We needed to do something. I told them it was bath time. As I bathed them silently, Anna Clare said, "I miss my Daddy so much, Mommy."

The tears I'd been holding back began to began to trickle down my cheek, "Me, too."

"Mommy you make me so sad," she continued.

"I know. Mommy's sad, too."

We all cried.

"But I want you to know," I said, "That it's okay to be sad. It's okay to cry. I also want you to know that now it's going to be Halley, Madison, Anna Clare, and Mom. We're going to have to be on our best behavior. We're going to have to take care of each other."

I looked at their tear-stained little faces in the tub. As sad as I was for myself, I felt even sadder for my children. I thought of my own father and how it always made me feel better just being in the same room with him. Safe, secure, unconditionally loved and cherished. My children would never again know the warm wonderful feeling that comes from having a dad's arms wrapped around them. Instead mine would long for his touch, his advice, his humor, and the memories they could have made with him.

I held them until they fell asleep in their beds.

It was almost 10 p.m. and there was still way too much commotion in the house. The doorbell continued to ring, as well as the telephone. Every few minutes I would hear the front door open and close, followed by the faint sound of footsteps and conversation. I needed the house to be quiet so the children could sleep.

The first thing I did was disconnect the phone in my bedroom. Then I went downstairs to the kitchen. I turned the other phone off. "There, that should help," I thought to myself. "Next, the front door."

Suddenly I realized my mom was sitting with neighbors in the family room. I couldn't believe I hadn't seen them there before. Not that it mattered. I was glad they were there. I offered a smile, but they didn't respond. They just stared at me. Then they stood and began making their way toward me. I heard someone call from the front door.

"Deena? Deena? It's me, Officer Stangle," said the voice.

I cracked the door open cautiously with the security chain still in place.

"Hi, Deena. How are you holding up?" said Officer Stangle.

"Okay, I guess."

He handed me several business cards from news reporters and said, "I know you're not going to like this, but the press are refusing to leave until you talk to them. Look."

I took the chain down and peeked out the door. Lit up by the flashing lights of squad cars, I could make out reporters and camera crews who seemed camped out on the lawn, standing by. A handful of police officers were trying to keep them at bay and neighbors were trying to assist.

I turned to Officer Stangle and said firmly, "They can stay out there all night for all I care. I am not going out there. Do you hear me? I am not saying anything. You heard what the FBI said."

About to cry again, I closed my eyes and covered my face to hold back the tears.

"I know. I know. But there's this guy we know really well. He works for the San Ramon Valley Times. He's a really nice guy. Do you think you could talk to him?"

"No," I said, my voice shaking. "Did you not hear what I just said?"

"Okay. Okay. I'm sorry, Deena. But I don't know what else to do. What do you want me to tell them?"

With tears welling, I said, "I don't care. Just tell them I've got nothing to say. Like I said, they can stay out there all night as far as I'm concerned." Then it hit me. "Tell them...Tell them I'm going to bed," I said, hoping that would work.

Officer Stangle seemed satisfied. I closed the door gently and turned around startled to find my mom standing before me with my neighbors right behind her. Without saying a word, Mon stepped forward, hugged me, and held me tight. Then my neighbors wrapped their arms around both of us. We all cried together.

"Deena, it's been a long day," said Mom, "Let's get ready for bed."

I nodded. Then I thanked my friends for coming when I needed them most.

As soon as they left, Mom and I went about the house turning off all the lights one by one, sending a clear signal we were going to bed. I went upstairs to check on the girls while Mom made ready to sleep on the couch downstairs. Surprisingly, the girls were sound asleep. In Anna Clare's room, I lifted the blinds hoping to see the news reporters leaving. Instead, I couldn't believe my eyes. Dozens of my neighbors and friends had joined together, holding hands to form a human barrier between my home and the media.

The night hours ticked by slowly. Well into the night, I still couldn't sleep. I lay in bed, watching footage of the day's horror: the planes striking the World Trade Center, the towers collapsing, the debris on the ground, the disbelief on the faces of survivors. I could not stop the thoughts swarming in my head.

I wondered what Tom's last few minutes must have been like. What had he been thinking? What had he seen and heard? How quickly did it all happen? Dear God, please let it be that he didn't have time to feel any pain as the plane ripped apart.

It was nearly 2:00 a.m. Tom's name scrolled across the bottom of the TV screen over and over: "Thomas E. Burnett, Jr. United Airlines Flight 93. Thomas E. Burnett, Jr. Plane Crash. Southeastern Pennsylvania. Thomas E. Burnett, Jr. United Airlines Flight 93. Plane Crash."

I can't sleep. Tom is supposed to be here. Tom is supposed to be home right now, sleeping beside me.

I wondered if the reporters were still outside. I didn't want to look.

I thought to myself how I had lived this day over and over in my imagination, hundreds of times, every time Tom left on a business trip. My worst fear always had been that he wouldn't come home. Was this that for which God had been preparing us –preparing me – all these years?

God knew I would need to draw strength from Him to endure this nightmare.

I tried to close my eyes, hoping to forget, but instead imagining the last moments of Tom's life filled my mind. I dreaded sleep, but I needed it desperately.

It was close to three in the morning. The night seemed never-ending and yet I didn't want morning to come. My mind turned to protocol. I remembered how Tom's dad had been upset when a close friend of his had died, and a family member hadn't contacted him.

"Should I start calling people before they hear about Tom's death on television?" I thought.

I grabbed my address book and picked up the phone, but came to my senses before I dialed. No one would be awake at this hour. I made a mental note to do it in the morning.

Then I laid back and tried to fall asleep, but it was no use. I was consumed with thinking about Tom. The cell phone calls. The unfairness of a young promising life snuffed out too soon.

I continued to drift, but sleep never came. The kids would be up soon. September 11, 2001, had been Tom's last. It had also been my first in the lifetime of days which lay ahead without him. The thought was more than I could bear.

Chapter Six

The Right Thing

*"Let us have faith that right makes might, and in that faith
let us to the end dare to do our duty as we understand it."*
– Abraham Lincoln

If Tom were alive today he'd laugh at the idea of being called a hero. He would tell you he was just doing the right thing.

Many today believe that there is no absolute right or wrong. If this were true, then we would have no heroes. Our concept of the word "hero" contains within it the assumption that this individual has chosen to do the right thing in difficult circumstances. It is precisely the accomplishment of this right thing at the right moment, which had earned the individual the title of hero. Implied then is that in a given set of circumstances there is a right thing to do. This means right and wrong are not relative. What seems right for you is not right for just you and what seems right to me is not right for just me. There are some things that *are* right and some that *are* wrong.

I believe each of us in the core of our being knows what these things are. For instance, we would never call one who has murdered in anger or for selfish reasons a hero. Yet we would call someone a hero who has killed in order to protect others. We know that what the Nazis did to the Jews during World War II was wrong. However, when the Allies stormed the concentration camps killing the Germans, we can all agree that this aided them in setting innocent captives free, which is right.

It is not that the passengers of Flight 93 took random action on September 11, 2001, which made them heroes, but that in our eyes, they did the right thing. Going forward, this is what each of us must seek to do everyday in our interactions. The right thing at the right time. Knowing it. Doing it.

Looked at another way, how could we hope to make good decisions if there was no absolute right and wrong? Against what standard could we weigh both sides in order to determine what was best, so we could move forward in confidence and conviction, ready to stand our ground, and even fight if it became necessary? What if during the 1930s and 1940s we had said, it may not be what we would do, but if it's what Hitler wants, then we're okay with that? Where would our world be today?

If we are to have a future, we must determine that which is absolutely right and do whatever we can to move its cause forward and protect it, just like the passengers of Flight 93. Just like Tom.

Generally like a hero's action, the right thing seems to be of less direct benefit to the one performing it and more for the benefit of a greater overall good. The wrong thing tends to put ourselves before the needs of others. However, where one would think that placing priority on ourselves would bring greater satisfaction than doing the right thing for others, it does not.

I believe this is because God is all good and can only bless that which is right. Thus, when we do what is good and right, our spirits are rewarded with hope and purpose. The wrong thing fills us with the opposite, i.e., ugliness and hatred, envy and anger, because the wrong thing is not of God.

Good acts are birthed from courage and conviction. Wrong acts are rooted in anxiety, fear, anger, and malice. Good and right acts stand firm and do what is right in spite of fear. The fear is still there, however, the individual is not controlled by it, but is spurred on to action by something greater.

All that said, doing that which is right and good is often not painless. Frequently it requires a conscious choice on our part to persevere through the "yuck" until the right thing is identified and accomplished. It is hard work and it's easy to become discouraged. We must keep our eyes on the goal – which is beyond ourselves.

Tom and his fellow passengers looked beyond themselves and did the right thing in the face of unanticipated, ugly circumstances which were beyond their control. Now, I stood on the threshold of a new life – one which I did not want. God had prepared the way. He set everything in place, to provide what I would need to get through. The choice was mine. Could I be courageous and step forward – doing the right thing – as Tom had done?

Deena Burnett with Anthony Giombetti

Chapter Seven

Standing Up, The First Step

" 'For I know the plans I have for you,' declares the LORD, 'plans to prosper you and not to harm you, plans to give you hope and a future.' " – The Bible, Jeremiah 29:11

September 12th

I didn't want to get up. If I just stayed in bed I could pretend none of the events of the previous day had happened. I knew that once I walked out that bedroom door, it would be all too real.

Then I remembered something Tom used to say. "You can be a victim or you can be a victor."

I had a choice. I could stay in bed, hide, and wither away. Or I could make things better. For the children, for Tom, I willed myself up. If Tom could do the right thing, so could I. I drew strength from my faith in God. He had shown me too much about how He had prepared me for this day. I didn't know how, but I would be okay.

I heard the girls outside my room and was glad for it. Mom was trying to keep them quiet so I could rest. I got up, walked out of the bedroom, saw the girls, and decided to keep them home from school. We would keep our day as uncomplicated as possible. They could spend the day in the safe cocoon of Mom's house. I would face my future. I would begin by addressing the media and telling the world about Tom. I had been worried about releasing information of Tom's phone calls, but everything I would have told the media had been reported on the news by the FBI, police, and Father Frank. If they could tell their stories, I knew now I could tell mine. There would be no harm to "the evidence" in answering their questions.

Mom was cooking breakfast and watching TV. She laid out the children's clothes on the sofa. I began dressing them. The phone rang. Mom must have plugged it back in. I answered. It was a reporter who said she was only a few minutes away.

"Do you mind if we do a quick interview?" she asked.

"My kids are here. But if you can do it outside, I'll give you five minutes." I didn't want my girls to hear.

I ran to the laundry room and grabbed a pair of jeans and a T-shirt. I quickly pulled my hair back. Barefoot and with no make-up, I walked outside to a clear, sunny day. She had already arrived with her cameraman.

I didn't care how I looked. Maybe it was because of yesterday's events. Then again, maybe it was because I was a mother of three children who had been up all night. It just seemed too trivial to matter anymore. I just wanted to get the interview over.

The reporter kept her word. She asked about the four calls, which Father Frank had told the media about the night before, then she wanted to know how the kids and I were doing. I summarized only the first call, and then briefly told her about the children and me. When I shared how Madison had asked if she still could call her dad on his cell phone, I noticed tears form in the reporter's eyes. But then, her five minutes were up. The interview was finished and she concluded by asking for a picture of Tom.

Not wanting her to enter the house, I closed the door behind me and rushed around to find a photo album. I thumbed through the pages, surprised at how few photos there were of Tom without the children. Eventually I found one and rushed outside. I showed it to her and the cameraman made a copy.

The interview had not been what I expected. It had not been as bad as I had imagined. She didn't pummel me with questions that I couldn't answer. She didn't make me feel bad. Seeing the reporter's reaction to my story also made me realize that other people outside my home had been affected deeply by what happened yesterday as well.

Back inside the phone rang again. A message was being left on the answering machine from *Larry King Live*. They wanted to talk to me. Calls from *People*, *Oprah Winfrey*, and *The Tonight Show* followed. They were all leaving messages, wanting to talk to *me*. I was incredulous.

And all of their messages began with the same sentiment. "First of all, I want to say I'm so sorry for your loss. My heart goes out to you, and our thoughts and prayers are with you. However, if you would be interested in doing an interview today, we would like you to go to the San Francisco affiliate or we could send a camera crew to your house..."

I was dumbstruck. Though some of the sentiments seemed heartfelt, most came across as empty words.

Seated at the table, Mom was trying to get me to eat, but I wasn't hungry. Even though I hadn't eaten anything in 24 hours, I had absolutely no appetite. So there I sat, listening to messages come in on the answering machine.

It just didn't stop. But it wasn't just the media. Strangers were calling, leaving messages. They were American citizens calling to offer their condolences. They always seemed to start their message with "Uhh, I hope this is the Burnett residence. I'm trying to reach the wife of the man who was killed on Flight 93..."

Since the outgoing message on our answering machine was non-descript, when people called, they weren't sure if they had the right number.

Most were calling to say thank you, telling me that my husband was a hero and that I must be so proud of him. One caller told how his 14-year-old daughter had been affected by the news story about Tom. At an age where most of her peers' heroes were pop stars or sports figures, the girl said she now hoped to be as courageous as Tom had been when she grew up. Another message from an elderly man said that if the children and I needed any financial assistance, to let him know.

Mom looked at me from across the table and asked, "Why did you decide to talk to the media? You know it's just going to make things worse."

I knew her intent was to protect me because she loved me, but I also knew she didn't understand yet what was fast becoming real to me. "Mom, I have realized I have to tell the story. What Tom did was an incredibly selfless act. People need heroes. They need someone to look up to. Tom should be that person."

I pressed on. "Not only did he die in a very honorable way, but he examined the life he lived. It was filled with integrity, truth, and honor. Look at the kids these days, Mom. They think how wonderful the lives of movie stars and professional athletes are. Then these so-called heroes are arrested for fighting, driving drunk, doing drugs, or beating their wives. These are not the role models our children need. They need men like my husband."

She still wasn't in total agreement with my decision, but she no longer tried to stop me.

"Deena, I'm just going to take the children to my house. You go ahead and do what you have to do."

As Mom prepared to leave with the girls, my Aunt Patsy arrived. I was glad to see her. "I tried calling all morning, but I couldn't get through," she said in a panic. "I thought I would just keep on driving from Modesto (which was about 90 minutes away). I knew you wouldn't be anywhere else but here."

I was relieved. I knew Aunt Patsy would be good for Mom. They could console each other and I could do what I needed to do knowing the girls were in good hands and in a safe place.

Just before nine o'clock, some of my friends arrived. They warned me that the media was beginning to gather on my lawn. To their surprise, I told them I had decided to talk to the press. Staunchly protective of me, they insisted on staying to offer their support. I assured them everything would be all right, but I was so very glad they were there.

These were some of my tried and true friends who I had known since Tom and I moved into the house five years ago. They were better than friends. They were like family. With but a few words spoken, they started rallying around the house, rearranging furniture, moving chairs, and clearing a large area. They put away the flowers and baskets of food left the day before by well-wishers. When the house was prepared, we opened the doors and into my small home filed dozens and dozens of reporters and cameramen.

We ushered as many as we could into the living room while I sat in the kitchen, waiting, watching strangers swarm into my home. I was protected behind the single wall downstairs so they could not see me until I was ready.

One of my friends stood like a sentry by my side, watching me intently. Another stood at the doorway. Others arranged chairs to accommodate the reporters' equipment. Still others ran back and forth between the living room and kitchen, re-affirming I still wanted to do this. I was amazed that no instructions were given and yet my friends knew exactly what to do.

For as many people that were in the house, the noise level was barely audible and the mood somber. All you could hear was the constant ringing of the phone. I decided to disconnect it again. As soon as I did this, one of my friends came into the kitchen and said, "They're ready."

Still wearing no make-up and my hair pulled back, I glanced at the faces of my friends and walked into the living room. Staring at a room full of strangers, I looked at them, and they looked at me. I didn't know what to say. They acted as if they didn't know what to say, either. I tried not to be afraid, but my heart was pounding. Then one of the reporters stepped forward, offering his business card and introduced himself. He extended his hand. I shook it while he told me how sorry he was for my loss.

Nodding politely, I stood there and tried to force a smile. *My mouth is never going to smile. I just know it. It feels so heavy.* I tried putting on a pleasant face while holding back the tears. It had begun.

One by one, the others followed suit. After introductions were made, I said with gesturing hands, "What do you want me to do?"

"Here," one of them said, sliding a dining room chair to the center of the room. "Here, please sit here."

I was glad to sit down. The lack of food and sleep were beginning to wear on me. Looking down, all I saw were feet. Everyone around me was standing, their cameras, note pads, and pens ready.

As I stared at the floor, I could only think, *This is not my life. What has happened?* I felt oddly disconnected from everything that was going on around me.

Then simultaneously they all started firing questions at me. It was too much at once. I couldn't understand any of them, so I didn't answer. I tried to look up, but the lights were so bright all I could do was blink. My eyes burned from crying and lack of sleep.

"We really should ask her one at a time," one of the reporters suggested.

Another said, "She can't see. Turn off some of these lights."

As soon as I was able I looked up and met their eyes. "You know, it feels odd to have all of you standing while I am sitting."

In an instant, everyone in the room crouched down at exactly the same time. On any other day I would have laughed out loud.

"OK, this is better," I thought, even though I still felt somewhat like a caged animal being watched.

The questions started again....This time, one at a time.

Their questions were emotionally charged and yet I couldn't feel anything in my reply. It actually amazed me that I was even able to speak. Nothing had prepared me for this. I relished my quiet life as a stay-at-home mom. I wasn't accustomed to speaking to groups of people, let alone in front of cameras.

On another day, I might have stuttered, or been unable to complete my thoughts. But now I had a purpose. I wanted to tell Tom's story in a way that would honor him. I spoke slowly and thoughtfully, carefully articulating what I wanted to say. So much had happened in the past 36 hours that there was no nervousness, only numbness and an incredibly in-my-bones sadness.

The first question was about the cell phone calls. My training as a broadcaster came in handy for my responses. I spoke in a deliberate, slow, and orderly fashion with many pauses, taking time to put a great deal of thought into my words before I uttered them. I had to be very cautious about everything I said. I didn't want to say anything that would interfere with the FBI investigation. I verified the calls had taken place, but gave no specific information about what Tom and I had discussed. I scarcely recognized the voice which came out of my mouth as my own.

Someone asked if I could hear anything in the background during the conversations. I decided to say no.

They moved on to Tom. A reporter wanted to know what he was like. What were his hobbies? What did I love about him? The mere mention of his name brought tears, so I stalled and tried to smile. I hadn't had the opportunity to talk to anyone about Tom. The FBI and police had not been interested in our relationship.

It was difficult to find the words because Tom meant so many things to me. I found it difficult to narrow my thoughts to a few sentences. But I tried, and it felt good to describe him.

"Tom was highly intelligent. He had a wonderful sense of humor."

Pause.

"He was a take-charge kind of guy who could motivate anyone to do anything he wanted them to do."

Pause.

"He was successful at a very young age because he was self-motivated and made smart decisions."

Pause.

"Tom enjoyed the outdoors, especially fishing and hunting."

Pause.

"He was athletic. He was a big guy who played college football and later enjoyed golf."

Pause.

"Where did he go to school?" a reporter asked.

"He earned his undergraduate degree at the University of Minnesota and received his master's degree from Pepperdine."

"Why was he in New York City and was he booked on Flight 93?"

"Tom was in New York on a business trip. As to the nature of his business, you'll have to talk to Thoratec – the company he worked for. And no, he wasn't booked on Flight 93. He was booked on a later flight, but changed his schedule to come home sooner. He had been traveling for several days and wanted to get home to his family as soon as possible."

The next question involved how the children were doing. I described in detail the conversation I had with them the night before, about their daddy not coming home. I told them about the children wanting to call his cell phone and write him letters. "They said they would miss his silly faces."

The room fell silent. Everyone seemed to struggle to hold their composure, until one reporter saw the silence as her opportunity and asked, "What has the world lost in your husband?"

I thought about how my mom had wanted him to run for President. I thought about the hundreds of people who had encouraged him to go into politics. I thought about how quickly he had risen up the corporate ladder and what a bright future and brilliant career he had in front him. I tried to find the words to be brief.

"The world lost a great resource in Tom Burnett. He was a brilliant man who had the potential for a brilliant career."

"What have your children lost?" continued the woman.

"My children lost a father and everything it means to lose a father."

"What have you lost?"

Her question made the weight of my grief almost unbearable. All I could manage to say was, "I lost a beautiful gift God gave me nine and a half years ago." I couldn't say anything else and lowered my head. The tears rolled down my cheek. One of my friends handed me a tissue. The reporters knew to stop.

When I looked up, I saw one of the cameramen crying. He got up and walked outside. It helped somehow to see that someone else could share some of my pain with me.

Three women approached. One of them knelt down and took my hand. She was a news reporter. She began crying then with a smile, stopped, and looked at me with gentle eyes. She said, "Mrs. Burnett, I just want to tell you that you are so sweet and kind, my heart just goes out to you. If there is anything, anything at all, I can ever do for you, please let me know." She scribbled down her name and number on a note pad, tore the sheet, and handed it to me. Then she walked away.

I didn't know who she was. But she was beautiful and her kind, kind words warmed my heart. It meant so much that she had taken the time to say them and I drew comfort from them.

The other two reporters offered their respects and left their business cards, saying they would pray for me.

After they exited, media wave two began. Again my friends were all over the place, directing traffic in and out of the house. As before, the reporters gathered in the living room while I sat in the center. They asked similar questions, wanting to know about the four cell phone conversations and what kind of person Tom was. I tried my best to answer them.

But as hard as I tried, I was unsure how successful I was. I wasn't thinking clearly. It was as though I was in a daze. All I could think about was that Tom wasn't coming home. Occasionally, right in the middle of a question, I would have to go to the kitchen to go over the notes I took when talking to him. Sometimes I couldn't even read the notes because my eyes still hurt so badly from crying and not sleeping.

Of the many faces staring at me in the living room, one of them looked vaguely familiar. Eventually I connected. She was Deborah Villalon from Channel 7. "She's the face I see on television every morning," I thought. "How strange. Now she's in my living room."

In walked Father Frank. He had a sparkle in his eye and a gentle smile on his face. He asked how I was doing. He embraced me as he planted a kiss on my cheek. The camera crews swooped in, surrounding us, at times right in our faces. Father Frank seemed to be playing to the media. I smiled to think of his amusement. Both our quiet lives had been disrupted, but he seemed to be enjoying it.

Meanwhile, my friend, Michelle, arrived. She came bursting through the crowded room, flinging her arms, completely indignant that the news reporters and cameras were in my house.

"Do you want me to get these people out of here?" she asked incensed.

"No, no. It's okay Michelle. I decided to talk to them."

Then she looked over my shoulder and noticed Deborah Villalon. Immediately she jumped between the camera and me and said, "Turn that damned thing off."

Her behavior caught me off guard, and I burst out laughing.

Michelle was from New Orleans. She was a true lady, but like most southern women she could bring out the cat claws when someone she loved was threatened. It felt good to have something to laugh about.

I asked Michelle to follow me into the kitchen. After a moment, she calmed down and said, "Well, I'm staying. I'm going to help."

The third media wave lasted about half as long as the first two. Maybe it was because their questions weren't as detailed or maybe I was getting better at answering them. It amazed me that I still wasn't nervous. But it wasn't because I felt in control. I was just too empty to feel anything.

During the fourth wave, I was asked to be on *ABC News Live* with Peter Jennings. Seated in the same chair, I now had an earpiece and a microphone creatively attached to my T-shirt. It felt as if wires were coming out of me in all directions. I could hardly move. When I did, even just slightly, they had to readjust everything.

The bright lights of the cameras continued to hurt my eyes. I kept blinking, and the burning formed tears. I was glad I didn't have on make-up.

While I waited to go on with Jennings, other news reporters approached, asking questions and videotaping me. Even though they came near me, I had a hard time hearing them. I kept hearing a voice in my ear from the ABC earpiece. It was confusing having so many people talking at once.

Twenty minutes went by and Jennings still hadn't interviewed me. They were experiencing difficulties with the satellite hook-up. Finally someone said it wasn't going to happen. They kept apologizing for having made me sit so long.

But I didn't care. I didn't have anywhere else to go. Nothing seemed to matter.

Then the ABC people told me Barbara Walters wanted to interview me on her morning show *The View*. I wasn't sure what they were talking about. None of this was making complete sense yet.

"That's weird," I thought. "Why would she want to talk to me?"

The producer asked if Barbara could call me. I nodded yes.

I received several phone calls from her staff, but never managed to return them. In fact, I didn't return anyone's phone calls. There must have been 200 messages that day, but the answering machine could only store 22 at a time and erased most of them before I could even listen to them.

By the last media wave, I had perfected my answers. I suppose I probably sounded monotone. I wasn't even listening to their questions anymore because I knew what they were going to ask.

The FBI returned around 3:00 p.m. and asked a few follow-up questions. Did I remember anything else? Did I want to tell them anything new? They said they needed a different phone number to contact Tom's boss, Keith Grossman, because he wasn't in town yet. I thought he would be at Thoratec, but it turned out he was in New York City. Until that moment I had not known that, as a result of the 9/11 attacks on our country, all airplanes across the United States had been grounded indefinitely.

The FBI also wanted the contact information for Tom's parents in Minnesota, Mrs. Bev and Mr. Tom, as well as to know who Tom's cell phone company was. The agents only stayed a few minutes and left.

After six full media waves, the press finally tapered off, stopping by only one at a time into the early evening, usually looking for photos of Tom. When the doorbell did ring, it was mostly friends offering their condolences and gifts. I gave the media photos that were taken in places Tom enjoyed. There was one of him fishing on Lake Hubert in Minnesota, another taken in Mexico. I even found one of him at a café in Paris, which I was able to share.

I had no regrets allowing the media in. Though then and in the months to come it was not always easy or convenient to be in the spotlight, I had made the decision to turn their interest in me to our mutual advantage. They could have the story, but I would tell it. No matter how painful it was going to be for me to remember that dreadful day, I didn't want anyone to ever forget what Tom and the others fought and died for. By choosing to be involved, I could ensure Tom's story was told correctly.

As evening came, my friends who had been such an invaluable blessing to me that day began to rightly turn their thoughts toward their own homes. They chatted about what they were going to cook for dinner since their husbands would be home soon.

Listening to them made me realize how different my life was. I should be the one worrying about what to cook for dinner. I glanced at the clock. If Tom were in town, he would be calling me on his cell phone right about now, saying he was on his way home. He would ask if I wanted anything from the grocery store. I'd tell him how much I missed him and ask about his day. He'd usually say, "Great. Busy, but great." We would talk about the girls and their day at school. Then, realizing he was just minutes away, I'd say, "Hey, we need to get off the phone. This is expensive. I'll see you soon." He'd laugh and say, "Okay. Okay." I fought back the tears knowing he wouldn't be coming home today.

The media left, my friends had gone home. I sat alone in my family room with only the incessantly ringing phone for company. I was alone and afraid. Nothing in my life seemed familiar anymore. I was no longer worried about the same things that preoccupied their minds. My whole life had been built around my marriage. Now, I was no longer married. I faced the new and unwanted challenge of finding a renewed sense of purpose. I was so weary.

It was such a welcome relief when Mom came in with the girls 20 minutes later. The kids came running in, and we kissed and hugged each other more tightly than ever. Never had we been more cognizant of the blessing of having each other. It was good to have them home. It was good to be together. Yes, we were sad. But we had each other.

Tom Burnett
May 29, 1963 – September 11, 2001

Photo by Barry Muniz

Deena Burnett

Tom at age five

**Tom played quarterback at
Bloomington Jefferson**

**The young Tom,
the first photo I
ever took of him**

Tom on Lake Hubert in Minnesota where he spent many summers as a child

This is my favorite photo of Tom. I snapped it one evening as I noticed him looking so lovingly at me.

Tom on a business trip in Honfleur, France. He enjoyed the region so much that we vacationed there a year later.

Tom and Deena marry on April 25, 1992

On our honeymoon in Aruba

Tom holding Madison and Halley at the farm house in Wisconsin

At home in San Ramon, Tom cradles Anna Clare

Saturday afternoon at the beach with Madison

December 24, 2000 – our last Christmas together

We spent our last weekend together camping at Mt. Shasta, CA

Memorial for Tom at the crash site in Shanksville, PA

Deena, Halley, and Madison at Tom's memorial service in California – four days after the plane crash

Deena at the California Day of Remembrance

The girls as flower girls at their Aunt Mary's wedding – eight weeks after their father died

Halley and Madison stand roses up-right so their father can see them from heaven

**Deena and the girls visiting President George W. Bush and
the First Lady Laura Bush at the White House**

Photo by Barry Muniz

Deena and the girls reminisce over photos of Tom

Chapter Eight

Putting One Foot
In Front of the Other

Have mercy on me, for in you my soul takes refuge. I will take refuge in the shadow of your wings until the disaster has passed. I cry out to God who fulfills his purpose for me.
— The Bible, Psalm 57:1-2 NIV

Outpouring of Love and Appreciation

Anyone can pray for peace, comfort, and strength. The difference is in whether you choose to allow God to give it to you His way.

As soon as the girls were out of range, Mom said, "Deena, those kids need you. They really, really need you. They don't need to be at my house. They need to be with their mother." Then she paused, her eyes swelling, and said, "Some of the things they said today touched my heart with such pain and sadness, I don't know where to begin."

Mom shared a conversation Aunt Pasty had with Halley and Madison.

"Did you know my dad died?" Halley told her.

"Yes, I know. I'm so sorry," said Aunt Patsy.

"But he's in Heaven right now."

"Well, that's a good place to be," responded Aunt Patsy.

"Yes, but it's so sad not to have a Daddy anymore."

"And if he was going away, why didn't he say good-bye?" asked Madison.

"I'm sure he didn't know he was leaving," said Aunt Patsy. "Sometimes when you have to go, it comes as a big surprise. And I bet that when your Dad realized he wasn't coming back, there probably wasn't time for him to say good-bye. I'm sure he misses you as much as you miss him."

I buried my face in my hands and wept, my body slumped, trembling. What heartache that my children would never know the comfort of having a relationship with a father. As I wept, an inner conviction of what I needed to do had begun to form in my mind.

It would be my responsibility to make sure the children knew Tom, whether he was here or not. It was important for them to know what kind of a father they had. I wanted the girls to know who he was and the principles for which he had lived. I wanted them to know that what he did on Flight 93 was the right thing to do – even though it cost him his life. Even though it cost us sharing that life with him. Most of all, they needed to know that just because he couldn't be with us, it didn't mean he didn't want to be there.

I went upstairs to where the children were. The atmosphere was so much more somber than usual. Normally, we played Barbie dolls or board games together. Sometimes we read books. But tonight I just sat on the floor and took turns holding them. I alternated putting my arms around one while the other two played quietly. We talked a little about their day.

Mom called us down for dinner. I watched the girls pick at their food. I couldn't eat either and my mom was giving us nervous looks. To relieve the pressure on her, I said, "Well girls, it's getting late, and you still need to take your baths. If you're finished, let's go." We headed back upstairs. My body was heavy with an intense weariness. The adjustment to Tom's death wasn't going to be easy for any of us.

When it was time for bed, they asked to say a prayer for Daddy. I saw an opportunity to offer comfort. "Of course," I said, "If you ever want to talk to Daddy, you could do so through prayer. Just ask Jesus to give him a message." And so we prayed.

I stayed with them again until they fell asleep. Since they had been up late the night before, it didn't take long. Downstairs, I found my mom in the living room, watching TV. The news showed clips of President Bush throughout the day. He looked different. His words were strong. His face was grave and sincere. At one point, he sat at a desk, vowing to make the situation right, promising to find out who was responsible for this destruction. Just listening to his strength and resolve made me feel better.

Because I had been isolated in my own shattered world the night before, I had not heard the predicted number of deaths from the September 11th attacks. The current estimate of those who may have died in the World Trade Center towers was 7,000. I felt nauseous and needed to leave the room. "Mom, I think I'm going to turn in for the night," I said, trying to hide my sick feeling. "It's been a long day."

The TV was off, the phone disconnected, and the girls fast asleep. The house was silent. With the girls in their beds down the hall, this time it was a good quiet. But for me, even though my body was beyond tired and I had a splitting headache, sleep would not come. I took an aspirin to ease the throbbing and decided to check messages on the answering machine to help the time go faster until hopefully I could fall asleep. Rather than disturb Mom, I brought the answering machine upstairs.

The answering machine took a while to rewind. The first message was from a man who said, "I'm just an American citizen who is really proud to live in a nation with men such as your husband." The next was from a lady offering to baby-sit. There were also several from widows who wanted to get together with me for coffee. But most were from ordinary people, citizens like me, who wanted to extend their condolences and offer prayers. These messages were from people all over the country.

I sat stunned in awe and disbelief as I listened to and cried through every single message. I tried to write them down so I would never forget the outpouring of their love to me – a stranger.

I was overwhelmed that these people had been so affected by Tom's actions on Flight 93. I was so glad they had taken the time to call. Their kind words meant a lot to me. But I wasn't sure how to respond. Over the weeks that followed there would be literally hundreds of messages, and I wanted each and every one to know how much they had touched my life with the brief words they had reached out to communicate.

I felt so very proud to live in this country, proud to be an American. It felt good to know there were still really good people in this world – people who cared, people who wanted to reach out, and made the effort to follow through.

After listening to the messages, I looked through photographs of Tom. The sleepless night hours were long and my imagination and thoughts ran the gambit. I imagined what the last few minutes of his life must have been like. What he must have thought, seen, and felt?

I was brought back to the countless times I had sat in the cockpit as a flight attendant, looking out the window during an airplane landing. Descending through the clouds, the ground would become closer and closer, the buildings and the trees growing larger and larger. With everything going on in trying to take over the plane, I wondered if Tom saw the ground approaching. I hoped that everything happened so fast he didn't have time to think about the impending crash.

The image of the crash site kept popping into my mind. The destruction had been so complete that there had been nothing recognizable. I worked to stop visions of Tom's body exploding which tried to take over my thoughts. I wondered what my beloved husband had felt as his body ripped apart instantaneously in a thousand different directions. How long did his pain last? How much of it did he feel? Then again, maybe he didn't feel anything. I prayed to God it was so.

What was it like when his spirit ascended from the earth? Did he look down, see the aftermath, and realize what had happened? Or did he simply have his face turned toward heaven?

A part of me had died with Tom. Though my spirit remained in my body, I knew he had carried our love, dreams, and happiness with him.

I felt so hollow, like a vast and desolate void. And if I couldn't feel anymore, if I was empty inside, why was I still here? How could I still be walking and talking when I felt so dead inside? I couldn't understand how someone in the condition I now found myself could still be physically alive. I had to do something. I couldn't just lie there. But I couldn't go outside my room, either. I couldn't go downstairs. I couldn't watch TV. If I did, I would wake up my mom and the children. I felt trapped in the bedroom Tom and I had shared for so many years.

I was beginning to dread the night. Unlike the day, which passed by quickly, the nights without sleep were long and painfully quiet. The darkness and stillness seemed to compound my own sense of emptiness. I desperately wanted someone to talk to, someone who would and could listen. All my friends had told me to call them if I couldn't sleep. But I didn't want to disturb anyone. I just needed something to do until the sun rose.

United Airlines had assigned a team of two people to our family, who were available 24 hours a day. I had questions and even though it was the middle of the night, I called them. The first thing I asked was Tom's seat number. They told me 4C. Because I couldn't seem to think straight, I said thank you and hung up.

A few minutes later, I called back. How many seats were in first class? "Twenty-four," they responded. Again I said thank you and hung up.

Since I had forgotten what kind of plane it was, I made another call. "What was the configuration of the airplane?" They said Flight 93 was a 757 with the seats in coach, three and three, separated by one aisle.

A little embarrassed, I decided to place one more call. "How many passengers were on board?" They said 44 people, including seven crewmembers and four hijackers.

With nothing left to do but watch the clock, I waited for the sun to rise.

As daylight broke on September 13th, the phone started to ring. This time radio stations were calling. As with the day before, reporters asked the same questions, and I answered them the same way. The radio interviews were much easier. After all, I could even do them from my bed and there were no cameras or reporters staring at me.

Because the phone kept ringing, and I knew the doorbell soon would start too, I decided to get out of the house and take the girls to school. It was important to return their lives to some kind of normalcy – if that was possible. We dressed and headed for San Ramon Valley Christian Academy in neighboring Danville. My mom went home for a change of clothes, planning to meet us back home around noon.

As I was backing out of the driveway, a news reporter began videotaping us. Before I knew what was happening, the girls rolled down their windows, stuck their heads out, and waved to the camera. I immediately stopped the car and jumped out. I did not want the children shown on television.

"Wait a minute!" I cried. "If you won't show my kids, I'll give you a few minutes."

They agreed. Standing in the middle of the street, I did a two-minute interview. The reporter asked how we were doing. I told her that our lives were filled with friends and family who loved us and that we had the prayers of a grateful nation. Under the circumstances, we were doing well.

I pulled into the parking lot at school. As was the daily custom, teachers, moms and dads, and children were assembling in the narrow courtyard where a flagpole stood tall bearing an American flag at half-mast. We gathered around with everyone else and waited for a morning prayer to be said, followed by the Pledge of Allegiance.

It didn't take me long to notice the many eyes staring at us. This was something I would have to get used to. We were different now. All of these women had husbands. I was a widow. Their kids had dads. Mine had a dad in heaven. The women were stay-at-home-moms. I would probably have to go back to work. I didn't like being different. It was uncomfortable.

The words of a teacher beginning to pray brought me back. She was praying for peace in the world and protection for us all. She prayed for the families who lost loved ones on September 11. She was talking about us.

To be prayed for in the presence of such a large group of people was a new experience as well. It felt awkward. I didn't want people to feel sorry for us. Not only had my life completely changed, but there within me something was changing as well. I could feel it, even though there were no words for it yet.

When it was time to say the Pledge of Allegiance, I looked up at the flag and was impressed in a new way of how beautiful this symbol of our nation was. It was as if even the flag had been changed by the events of the last few days. To me, it had never looked quite so vibrant or so purposeful before. I knew it stood for strength, and I fixed my eyes upon it, absorbing all the strength that I could. I saw with new depth the greatness of what it stood for: freedom, valor, honor. I thought about all the lives which had perished. Stricken with emotion, I was unable to speak.

The voices of these young children, pledging allegiance like a chorus to the liberty of our nation, filled my mind. Silently, I prayed for them to understand what they were saying. How important it was to mean what you say. I wanted them to appreciate the value and privilege of being raised in the United States. I wanted them to know how great our nation is, filled with opportunity and choice, a place where we have the privilege of choosing our career, our religion, and our education without the legislation of our government. Of all the nations in the world, I wanted them to know it is here where we have the greatest opportunity to live out in God's grace His plan for us. Most of all, I wanted them to know we have those privileges because men and women were willing to die for them. Because September 11 was being called an act of war declared on America, I knew my husband was now one of these patriots.

I kissed the girls good-bye and returned home. Several friends had already arrived. They were checking on me and asked how they could help. Reporters were to be turned away. I had answered all their questions the previous day, there would be no need for more interviews today.

Mid-morning, the school principal came by. At first I was alarmed. Was something wrong with the children? But she just wanted to know how I was doing.

I told her I had been unsure whether taking the girls to school was the right thing to do, but had decided it was a better place than home.

"I think you did the right thing," she responded both warmly and confidently.

Her assurance felt good.

"I checked in on the girls before I left," she continued. "I thought you'd like to know."

She went on to tell me that a few reporters had stopped by the school, but were turned away. "We didn't let them have access to the children," she said.

She handed me a list of moms who had set up a schedule to supply us with meals. I was to call and let them know what we needed.

She was a strong, gracious woman. Having her in my house brought great comfort. It was easy to see she cared deeply about the well-being of her students. I knew my girls were in the right place.

Three more friends joined us. Together, we sat around the kitchen table, sipping coffee, and talking about the events surrounding September 11. Though I wasn't interested in taking phone calls, my friend handed the phone to me anyway. It was our church calling. I excused myself. They were checking to see what my plans were for Tom's memorial service.

Her question caught me off guard. I had been dealing with a terrorist attack and plane crash. I hadn't even thought about a memorial service. Turning to my friends, I asked their advice. They suggested that since Tom's actions had affected so many, it might be healing to the entire community to hold a public service.

They gave me an initial glimpse of what was going on in the United States beyond my home. They explained how stores were sold out of American flags. Many were flying flags from the back of their pick up trucks or were standing on street corners and overpasses waving the flag and shouting U.S.A. Others had banners and signs with

Tom's name on them, thanking him for what he had done. Patriotism was surging across the country. Americans were hurting, but the experience was bringing them together. I learned of candlelight vigils, prayer meetings, worship services, moments of silence, and people raising money to help the families. Even people in other countries had been inspired by the actions of Flight 93 to fight back on their own turf.

Hearing this and considering the hundreds of phone calls, messages, letters, and flowers I had received from family, friends, and strangers, I got my first inkling of the huge extent to which the world had been affected by the tragedy. Could something positive actually come from the pain and loss we were suffering? Could a public memorial service for Tom help in some small way? It wouldn't take away my pain, but it would be nice if something good – however small – could come from this horrible time.

I took a moment to call Tom's parents, Mr. Tom and Mrs. Bev, in Minnesota. They had received a call from their church, St. Edward's, as well. We quickly agreed that it would be best to hold two memorial services: a public service at our parish in California this week and a private service at St. Edward's the following Monday. Everyone at my kitchen table enthusiastically offered to help.

At first St. Isidore's was unable to accommodate us. It was already Thursday and the church was booked for other functions on Friday and Saturday. Besides, 24 hours was too short a time period within which to plan a memorial, they said.

Disappointed, I began thinking a California service wasn't going to work out. But to my surprise, the church called back 15 minutes later and said it was possible.

They explained that President Bush had just issued a statement announcing that at noon on Friday, September 14, the nation would observe a moment of silence. St. Isidore's said they decided to honor the President's request by holding a special service during that time of day – a memorial service, honoring Tom.

They immediately sent people over to help with planning. We had exactly 24 hours.

It's amazing what happens when something is ordained by God. Though everything initially looked a little shaky, it all ended up falling into place beautifully.

Father Frank, along with the pastor and the appropriate parish committee head helped with all the details. After some discussions regarding which Scriptures to use, I told Father Frank whatever he wanted to do was fine with me. "I have a few people in mind for the eulogy and scripture readings," I said. "Otherwise, everything else is up to you."

He pressed me whether I had any musical preferences. The only songs I could think of were Amazing Grace and How Great Thou Art.

He laughed and said, "Oh Deena, those are Protestant songs."

"Well, yes they are, I grew up Protestant," I smiled.

Then I remembered Ave Maria. Tom loved that song. In fact, he wanted it sung at our wedding. I couldn't find a singer who could do it justice in such a small town. So he had said, "Then we'll save it for my funeral." I was glad I remembered. Now he would have it. Quickly, it was settled.

At noon, the girls came home from school, and we had lunch in our backyard in the warm California September sun. We continued to experience an increasing amount of random acts of kindness from people we'd never met before. For example, an eleven-year-old boy stopped by. He carried a large American flag on a pole that he must have taken off the side of his house. "Ma'am, I'd really like to do something nice for your girls. Do they like Barbie dolls?"

I wasn't sure what to say. All I could do was nod yes.

"Okay Ma'am," he said and left. He returned within the hour with gifts for each of the children. This time he introduced himself as Nick, the son of one of my neighbors. And sure enough, he had Barbie dolls and Barbie doll clothes for each of the girls. As he turned to leave, I was overwhelmed. What could I say, but thank you?

"Anything I can do, Ma'am," he replied over his shoulder.

Standing at the front door, I watched him walk away until he was out of sight with his huge flag waving atop his school backpack.

Throughout the afternoon, the girls played with their new toys while I kept busy doing what I could for the memorial service. I only answered my cell phone. I knew anyone calling that number would be someone with whom I wished to speak. I let the answering machine take care of the rest.

All news reporters that dropped by were turned away. Two employees from Tom's office volunteered to sit in their car outside my house and tell each reporter I was unavailable. I had said everything I wanted to say. Any other information I had from those calls was just for me to know.

At the time, I really had intended to set aside only that one day to talk to the media, hoping that would be enough. It was a naïve plan, but in the end it worked out.

With the media held back and the memorial service being planned by the church officials, I turned my attention to traveling to Minnesota. The Burnetts wanted us there as soon as possible. They even suggested the girls and I take a train if flying was too stressful. I considered it, but heard on the news that an Amtrak train had derailed. Nothing looked safe, and I was in no condition to drive. We had to fly.

Newscasters had been speculating that airports nationwide would re-open on Friday or Saturday. With the Burnetts planning a Monday memorial service, that meant we would have to fly out sometime during the weekend, in order to arrive in time for their memorial.

I turned my attention to packing and realized I had nothing appropriate to wear to my own husband's services. I mentioned this to Beth, one of the Thoratec employees. She promised to take care of it. Later that afternoon she arrived at our home with armloads of coordinated new suits, dresses, shoes, hosiery, bows, and accessories from Nordstrom's for all of us. "They sent all of this over for you to choose from. They said to keep whatever you want, no charge."

I was astounded. I asked Beth and Monica, who had been keeping me company, to help me decide. They chose a blue suit.

I never wore this color. My closet was filled with black clothes. I also thought it might be disrespectful to not wear black to my husband's funeral. They insisted it was the best choice, and I didn't have the energy to fuss about it more. I was just thankful God had provided a way for me to look presentable.

For each suit, there were matching dresses for the children. I laughed, thinking how Tom hated for the children to dress alike. He was adamant about allowing them to develop their own personalities. He thought if we insisted they always look the same, it made it that much harder for them to develop their own likes and dislikes.

After setting aside a few different suits and dresses, knowing there would be a number of functions to attend while in Minnesota and with no time to shop, Beth reminded me that Nordstrom's said to keep whatever I wanted. "It's on the house," she said. "There's even a thank you note to Tom." It said, "Thank you for your sacrifice."

This was the first of many very generous gifts. In each case, it was difficult to graciously accept them. I was accustomed to being the giver, the one to take meals to friends when they were sick, or to baby-sit children when their parents needed a break. Now everyone else was doing these things for me. It happened with such frequency, there is no way I could list all those who helped me during this difficult time. There were more examples than can be mentioned.

For instance, the local Volvo dealership learned from Officer Stangle on September 11th that my car was broken down 30 miles from home. They had it towed, repaired, and delivered to my home overnight for free. The Ford dealership learned my husband hadn't followed up on their offer to sell us the Expedition because he had died. They gave me the car so I would have something reliable for the girls and myself. One time after I had learned that we had not pre-paid the girls' private school tuition prior to Tom's death, I despaired where I would find the thousands of dollars to keep them in the school. Out of the blue, one of my friends dropped by a laundry basket filled with cards from well-wishers. In opening the cards, I found enough money to more than cover the tuition expense. Then a friend anonymously paid for Anna Clare's pre-school tuition. I found myself crying not only because Tom was gone, but also because of how kindly I was being treated, and how

God was providing for our needs through the goodness of strangers. I didn't know how to say thank you.

Though words seemed grossly inadequate to express my heartfelt, sincere appreciation for the kindness that was being shown to us, it was all I had. I didn't have the energy or resources to do anything else. And so I said thank you over and over again. Thank you, thank you, thank you. In fact, those words became such an automatic response that by the end of the day, my friends were poking fun at me because I was saying thank you to things where it wasn't necessary.

That night we retired exhausted again. To keep myself busy when sleep eluded me, I began to go through the mail which was pouring in. The first letter I opened was from a woman whose son worked at the White House. She wrote how grateful she was that her son was alive because of my husband's sacrifice. The second one was from a lady who said what a wonderful man my husband must have been to take the kind of action he did on Flight 93. She believed that he was a tribute to our family, his parents, and his upbringing. The third letter was from a man who said he hoped that he would have done the same thing in Tom's place. He wanted me to know how grateful he was for Tom's actions because his children now knew true heroes existed. Sitting on the floor, I read letter after letter, over and over, trying to find comfort.

I noted the return addresses. These letters were coming in from all over the country – Georgia, New Mexico, Alaska, Maine, and Massachusetts. I still couldn't believe the outreach from so many people who were touched by our circumstances. After I finished reading them, I got the answering machine and played the messages over and over, thinking about Tom. I cried until there were no more tears.

I was so weary, I almost couldn't move. But I still couldn't fall asleep. Every time I closed my eyes I would see him in the cockpit of that airplane. So I stared at the ceiling and listened to the silence. Another night which seemed to go on forever.

California Memorial

When morning came, I was restless. Anxiety about the memorial service at St. Isidore's was building.

My mother's relatives arrived from the San Joaquin Valley, a two-hour drive east from San Ramon. We did not know each other well, but I was thankful for the effort they had made to come support me during this difficult time. I wanted to be a good hostess and engage them in conversation while we waited for it to be time to go to the church, but I was drained, physically, emotionally, and mentally. All I could do was think about Tom.

I had in my mind to be strong for the memorial. I wanted everyone to know that regardless of how horrible the situation was, we were going to be okay. I knew it in my heart. I needed to prove this to others by not crying, by not breaking down. I had to find a way of saying, "I know the situation is bad, but we're going to survive it."

It was time to go. The limousine was waiting outside. It was the same car service that had always taken Tom to the airport. The ride to and from the memorial was their gift to us and it was appreciated.

Outside the security gate to our community, there was a small memorial growing in Tom's honor. I could see American flags, pictures, banners, and candles. One sign read, "Tom Burnett, American Hero."

We arrived at the church a few minutes early and parked out front. I didn't want to get out. I wanted to wait until the very last minute before going in. We sat in the car quietly and watched hundreds of people pour into the church. The large numbers surprised me.

The seemingly endless sea of faces reminded me of a conversation Tom and I had had several years ago about a funeral he attended for one of his co-workers. The man had died of cancer. Such a huge number of people attended his funeral, that it was "standing room only." Tom was impressed. During the service, story after story was recalled about how this man had opened his heart and home to hundreds of people in need. His children's friends were always made to feel welcome and his kindness had always preceded him. Tom told me he hoped to lead the kind of life that would call for a "standing room only" funeral as well. I sat there wishing he could see the crowds who had come to honor him.

It was time to go in. I got out, taking the children by hand. When I reached for Anna Clare, she pulled away and screamed, "No, no, I don't want to hold your hand." I was taken back at her sudden outburst. I tried not to let it turn into an ordeal. I took the hands of Halley and Madison. My mom reached for Anna Clare.

We walked up the steps into the vestibule, followed by our relatives. Inside the sanctuary, which could comfortably seat 3,500 people, it was indeed standing room only. Extra chairs had to be brought in for people standing in the aisle. The thousand who couldn't be accommodated found themselves standing outside looking through the windows.

The music began to play. We were led down the aisle. I was still holding Halley and Madison by the hand. My mom, Anna Clare, and the rest of the family marched behind in procession. We were led to the front row where we filled the first four rows.

Halley, Madison, and I knelt to pray. After a long pause, I raised my head. Tom's photograph sitting near the altar came into view. I sighed deeply and the tears flowed. Halley and Madison noticed their dad's picture too. They gripped my hands more tightly, realizing it wasn't a normal church service. "Why is Daddy's picture up there?" asked Halley. "Yeah," said Madison, "Why are we here Mommy?"

Little teardrops glistened in the corners of their eyes. I reached over and tucked them closer to me as we sat back "We've come to say good-bye to Daddy," I said. "Even though he's in Heaven, we are going to talk about how wonderful he was and how much we will miss him." Madison started to cry. I tried to comfort them both by putting Madison in my lap and holding on to Halley with an outstretched arm.

Cameras flashing on the far left side of the room drew my attention. *What are they doing here!* My temperature began to rise, but then I remembered the church memorial coordinator had asked me yesterday if I minded cameras at the service. Since I felt so incapable of making a decision, I asked her to decide. Now I had my answer.

I turned my attention back to the girls, then to Tom's picture. I was now staring at it. As hard as I tried not to, tears streamed down my face. I told myself to be strong. I concentrated on being glad that I chose that particular photo of Tom. He looked so happy. I tried to imagine that expression on his face as he entered Heaven.

The service started. The Bishop and all the priests sat behind the altar. Several dignitaries and politicians were seated to my left. Most of the service disappeared in a blur, except the Ave Maria. It was sung beautifully and made my heart lighten.

Near the end of Mass, two close friends of Tom recalled fond memories of him. The first was Diane Perro, a college classmate at the University of Minnesota; the second was Tom's boss and best friend Keith Grossman. Keith's eyes had tears in them, causing him to pause in the beginning. It seemed unlike Keith to be so emotional. I didn't know him very well, but always saw him as being strong and unapproachable. He'd known Tom longer than I had. They had worked together at three different companies and between travel and the office, Keith easily spent more time with Tom than I did.

He delivered a beautiful eulogy by using the most perfect words to describe Tom. I even laughed a few times at some of the things he said. I was so glad Keith was able to articulate who Tom was and the character he possessed.

When he finished, the service was over. The children and I were escorted up the aisle toward the entrance. With each step, my feet grew heavier. The small hands of my children's inside mine steadied me. Along the way, thousands of faces stared at me from both sides of the church. I wasn't sure if I recognized anyone because my eyes were so glazed with tears. As much as I wanted to, I couldn't look into their faces. And so I kept my eyes forward.

Once outside, I descended the church steps and made my way across the street to the reception hall. There, to my pleasant surprise and great relief, the ladies from my Ministry of Mothers group were there to greet me. To have them standing in front of me meant more to me than anything else I could imagine at the moment. We knew each other so well, I didn't have to explain anything to them – not my love for Tom, the loss I felt, or the pain I was suffering. They already knew. We hugged and cried together before the crowd rolled through the doors. Then a church representative interrupted and asked, "Mrs. Burnett, there are going to be people who want to talk to you. Do you mind standing across the room over there, so that as people come in, they can cross the room to speak to you? Otherwise, they will have to stand outside in a line."

I was surprised to hear that people wanted to talk to me, but was happy to oblige. Those few minutes with my M.O.M.S. group before the doors opened calmed my nerves and renewed my strength.

Though a well-provisioned buffet table awaited the guests, very few seemed interested in eating. They came straight to me. Most people were unable to say anything. They just stood in front of me and cried, hugged me or held my hand, then walked away. Some handed me a note scribbled on the back of their business card. Others recited beautiful poems, telling me how grateful they were for what Tom did.

There were pilots and flight attendants dressed in uniform. There were people that Tom and I had met at different places, at different times in our lives: schoolteachers, attorneys, real estate agents, housewives, construction workers, and local grocery store cashiers. And there were strangers, people who drove hours just to be there and say thank you.

Watching the line grow outside the reception hall, I wondered if everyone was in a state of shock about what happened to our country. I sensed their deep sorrow and need to begin healing. I thought perhaps they just wanted a connection with someone who had been killed. Maybe Tom's memorial was helping to make that possible.

Two hours passed and the line was still too long for me to see the end. A friend of mine, afraid that I might pass out since I had hardly eaten or slept in four days, slipped a chair underneath me. It was appreciated. I had lost 10 pounds in four days and exhaustion was taking its toll.

An announcement was made that the church's school was letting out and the parking lot needed to be cleared. The remainder of the "receiving" line dispersed, and I noticed Keith standing before me with his wife, Hallie. Keith handed me an envelope and said, "You don't have to read it now. Wait until you feel up to it." He also handed me Tom's paycheck receipt. (Under Keith's direction, Thoratec continued to pay Tom's salary until the life insurance and death benefits were paid. Because the checks were direct deposit, I didn't realize he was still on the company's payroll for several months. I thought the receipt I was given at the memorial service was the last to come.)

"You and I need to sit down and talk," he said. "I know that you're not going to want to do that today or tomorrow or maybe not even next week, but it needs to be done and as soon as you are able. I'll go over everything for you so you'll know where you stand and what needs to be done." He didn't say it, but I knew he was talking about finances.

All I said was, "Okay".

Keith looked at me as if there was something else he wanted to say. I eased the awkward silence by thanking him for his kind words about Tom and for being at the service. Keith had been stranded in New York and had to charter a plane to get home in time for the memorial.

Finally, Keith said what was on his mind. "Deena, I want you to know that you're going to be OK. You're not going to have to worry about a thing. I'm going to make sure that everything's taken care of."

I nodded my head.

Then he asked, "Do you need anything? Anything at all?"

"No. I'm all right."

"Deena, I want you to know that we have a lot of resources, and we can help you with whatever you need. Whether it's cleaning out files or going through the mail or sending out thank you notes, whatever it is you need, just let me know. And we'll take care of it."

I searched his face and wondered what Tom would have said to Hallie had Keith been killed. While they didn't look alike, their mannerisms, their voice, and their words held striking similarities. Today I saw a gentler side to Keith than I think even Tom had known.

"Thank you, Keith," I responded. "I'll be on your doorstep if I need anything."

He smiled and said, "No you won't, Deena. I know I'll have to come to you."

Tom must have shared more about me to Keith than I realized. I knew he was right. I would never ask anyone for anything.

Back home, I could barely get into the house. Flowers, gifts, and letters filled the walkway and porch spilling onto the front yard. The girls kept wanting to know if it was a holiday. My mom and relatives were already inside trying to put everything away. I was glad to see my mom's family was able to stay a little longer. With the strain of the memorial passed, we sat down and visited for the next two hours while the children played with their cousins in the backyard.

That evening we were invited to dinner at Monica's. We were already an hour late when we left our house. I had been to Monica's hundreds of times, but tonight I couldn't remember how to get there. My mind was mud. I made several wrong turns and had to stop and turn around several times. I wish I hadn't turned down her offer to pick us up. I thought we were never going get there. I pulled over and said a short prayer to have the ability to focus on what I was doing. It took me 45 minutes to make a 10-minute drive.

I have been to dinner parties by myself many times. Tom's travel schedule often kept him away. But tonight it didn't feel right. Monica had her husband Allen. Michelle was there with her husband Mike. I was alone. To be around couples and not be a part of one any more made me feel out of place. I tried not to let it show.

During dinner, Michelle's husband Mike said he heard that Congress was considering giving Tom and others on Flight 93 the Congressional Medal of Honor. I broke down and began to cry.

After I had time to collect myself, the conversation then turned to how September 11th was changing our country. Like a spectator at a play, I listened to the men discuss how our entire nation was in a state of shock. People at work were in a daze and unable to concentrate. Even those with no personal connection were grieving our nation's loss.

I found this interesting. Why would everyone be in such a state of shock? I knew why I was in my condition. I had lost a husband. Who had they lost? Slowly but surely my eyes were being opened that September 11th meant the world outside my home as well as in it had irreversibly been changed.

Minnesota Day of Remembrance and Memorial

Back home I settled the children into bed. In the morning we were leaving for Minnesota. Tom's sister Mary and her fiancé, Chad, had flown in to accompany us so I didn't have to fly alone with three young children. I still wasn't sleeping so I passed the time packing. It took me all night to decide what we needed. I wasn't thinking clearly. Many times I would put something in a suitcase and forget it was there. Then I would search around the house for it, not realizing it had already been packed. Finally I gave up, threw a few things in, and closed the suitcase.

Soon the house began to stir, and I was feeling wary about flying. On the way to the airport, the fear inside me grew. I didn't voice my concern, but the kids could sense it. "Mommy," said Madison, "if no one was paying attention when the bad people got on Daddy's plane, why do you think they'll pay attention when we get on the plane?"

I was stunned by her young insight. "They have extra workers at the airport now, honey," I answered. "There are special people who check everyone's bag."

"How will we know if there are bad people on our plane?" asked Halley.

"Yeah, and what do they look like?" chimed Madison.

I tried to reassure them, but didn't think I was very convincing. Stressed, I put my trust in God. *If it's our time, then it's our time. At least if the plane goes down, we'll all be together.*

I was out of answers, and I couldn't keep the children from being afraid so I told them I had a great idea. "Let's say a prayer and ask God to keep us safe today. Okay?"

The prayer calmed them, and the questions stopped.

When we arrived at the airport, Northwest and United Airlines personnel greeted us and escorted us directly to our gate. This was a great relief because the lines were terribly long. United had arranged for us to fly non-stop on Northwest so we wouldn't have to worry about connections.

Since there was still time before the flight took off, we waited in their frequent flyer room. Sitting there, exhausted, I watched Mary and Chad play with the girls and give them cupful after cupful of cola. The children were buzzing all around the room, being children and it was comforting to watch.

Anna Clare was still behaving strangely toward me. When I tried to read her a book, she wouldn't come near. "Give her time," I thought. "Give her time."

I picked up the San Francisco Chronicle. This was the first time I had read any print news coverage about September 11. To my surprise, there were many stories about Flight 93. They even used Tom's picture. I decided to keep the newspaper.

After being in the frequent flyer lounge for over an hour due to flight delays, I turned to Chad and Mary and said, "Hey you guys, I have a tip for you to file for future reference."

"Oh, what's that?" said Mary.

"When traveling with children, especially on an airplane, don't fill them full of caffeine and sugar prior to boarding."

They turned to each other with a puzzled look, which faded to embarrassment. They had not even considered how much energy they were pumping into the children.

"But they looked so sad," said Mary apologetically. "We just wanted them to be happy." Then she laughed out loud and said, "Oh no, what have we done?" In a hopeless effort to fix the problem, she immediately began pouring out the drinks and tried to persuade the girls that water was better. Even though I was worn out, I managed to laugh.

At boarding time Halley, Madison, and Anna Clare froze at the entrance to the airplane. They stood silent and would not budge. I knew they were afraid. Reaching down, I picked up Halley and Madison, one under each arm, and carried them onto the plane. When I returned for Anna Clare, she wouldn't let me pick her up. She started screaming, "No, No!" and went running back up the jet way. Chad chased after her, finally caught her, and gently persuaded her to board the plane.

We sat one adult per child. As the plane prepared to take off I was extremely nervous. I listened to every sound and only relaxed a bit when the wheels went up. I looked around to see if there were any people of Middle Eastern descent on board. Then realizing what I'd done, I was ashamed.

I didn't like how I was thinking. I tried to put those thoughts out of my head by falling asleep as we ascended into the sky and managed to for a few minutes before being awakened by the seat belt sign going off. The flight attendants knew who we were and called us by name. They each introduced themselves and offered their condolences. They thought Tom was a hero. It was nice to have everyone be so kind.

The flight attendants were also generous with their time toward the children. They played and talked with the girls. They colored pictures together and let them go in and out of the galleys. This made it easier for me to rest a little. But I only sat there with my eyes closed, still not sleeping.

When we arrived at the Minneapolis St. Paul International airport, Tom's parents, Mr. Tom, and Mrs. Bev, as well as his older sister, Martha, were there to greet us. I looked into their faces to see if theirs had been changed like mine. I couldn't tell.

Our Minnesota itinerary was full. That afternoon was to be the Minnesota Day of Remembrance on the steps of the State Capital. We would go to the hotel later that evening to greet family members arriving from all over the country. The memorial would follow on Monday.

The family reminisced about seeing Tom the previous weekend. "He seemed so happy," said Mrs. Bev. "Tom was supposed to spend Saturday night at the farm in Wisconsin, but instead he came back early to be with us. We were so glad to have that evening together. That night will always be precious to us."

Being around people who knew Tom, who really knew him, helped put me at ease. Even though my friends in California were constantly by my side, none of them knew Tom the way his family did. Until now, I hadn't felt comfortable talking about him or sharing memories. It felt good to be with his family. There was something healing about being able to laugh and cry together without having to explain. We remembered Tom with poignant moments, smiles, laughter, and good conversation. Being able to talk about Tom and remember him in such a pleasant and emotionally complete way brought some needed relief from all the pain.

While the Burnetts continued to reminisce about their last weekend with Tom, I did the same, but inwardly. I also thought of all our good conversations. I remembered how we met and the things we did before having children. I remembered our weekend trips. I even thought about the times we just sat at home and watched television. And in particular, I remembered the day Tom proposed and the day Anna Clare was born. God had worked to prepare me in advance for this.

Sitting at the kitchen table, I found myself trying to make sense of it all. I wanted to put everything into some kind of order, but it was too soon. I tried to find a way to come to terms with what had happened. But the wound was still too raw. I let go of these thoughts, excused myself, and went upstairs to rest. The Minnesota Day of Remembrance was only a few hours away.

The girls stayed behind with their aunt and uncle while the rest of us went to the Minnesota State Capitol in St. Paul. One family at a time, we were taken to meet Governor Jesse Ventura and his wife, Terry. I had been looking forward to meeting her. I had seen a television interview with her not long after she became First Lady of Minnesota. Although she seemed quiet and shy, she appeared genuine and I liked her.

When I met the Governor, for some reason I became emotional and felt like crying. Even though I held it together, I was unable to speak.

So we shook hands. When he reached down to hug me, I reached up and whispered, "I remember seeing an interview with your wife. She said she had been cast into a role she was not prepared to play. I feel the exact same way today."

He stood back with a confused look and said, "What? What did you say?"

I couldn't hold back the tears any longer. Mrs. Ventura approached to comfort me. As best I could, I said the same thing to her. "I feel as if I've been cast into a role I'm not prepared to play."

Tears formed in her eyes. Silently, she grasped my hand. She had grown into her role so beautifully, I hoped I would too.

I left the room and took my ceremonial seat for the Minnesota Day of Remembrance. The Burnetts and I had been asked to place a wreath in the center of the seating area located on the State Capitol steps. Afterwards, we said the Pledge of Allegiance. Never before had the words of the pledge had such personal meaning for me.

After the ceremony, Mrs. Bev and I were briefly separated from the rest of the family. Standing against the wall in a corridor, I waited for the crowd to thin out. Mrs. Ventura happened by. She saw me too and came toward me. We hugged. She took my hand and said, "Some day, you'll grow into your role the way I did, and you'll do a great job." Her words were balm to my heart.

Soon thereafter we went to the hotel where all the families were gathering. I saw my dad there for the first time. How wonderful that was! He was the one person in my life who was always a good listener.

My aunts and uncles, brother and sister, and many more relatives were there. They had given up a lot to make this trip. Most of them, hardworking people who were paid by the hour, had to take several days off work without pay to make the drive up for the Memorial.

I also met many of Tom's relatives for the first time. In particular I sought out Tom's cousin Paul, who was a pilot for American Airlines. I was still searching for more answers about the crash. I needed to know from him if he thought Tom could have flown the plane after wrestling it from control of the terrorists. He assured me Tom could have – if he had time before it was too late.

It was getting close to the girls' bedtime. Rather than drive all the way back to the Burnett's, my step-mom and dad offered to keep them at the hotel. The girls were thrilled. Once they were bathed and in bed, I returned to the Burnett's. I still hadn't eaten more than a few bites all week.

I knew the kids were safe and well cared for, so I took a sleeping pill. It enabled me to sleep for three hours. I awoke around one o'clock in the morning, thinking of Tom and what I needed to do the next day.

Before turning off the light and trying to sleep again, I decided now would be a good time to read Keith's letter. It touched me deeply. As Tom's closest friend, Keith affirmed everything I had loved and known about my husband. In it, Keith also reiterated his promise as Tom's most trusted friend to be available to me in any way I might require assistance.

I was still far from being myself. It took me all Sunday morning just to take a shower and get dressed before leaving for the hotel. We met my family for lunch; I spent time with the girls. My afternoon would be spent at St. Edward's, helping plan the memorial. Tom's sisters Martha and Mary were already at the church. I was glad they were taking the lead on planning the service because everything, even the smallest things, felt like an incredible task to me.

Sitting in church, joined by Monsignor Joe, we went over Scriptures and readings. The Monsignor had always been a part of the family. Mr. Tom and he had grown up together in Mason City, Iowa. He always performed the family weddings and baptisms and was a precious part of our lives. He had even traveled to Arkansas to perform our wedding. None of us had expected to need him to perform a funeral so soon. Monsignor Joe made several suggestions for the ceremony, though I must admit that I wasn't paying much attention until I heard the word *doves*. Monsignor Joe said something about releasing doves at the memorial service. Mary and I looked at each other, and she said, "I can just hear Tom saying, 'No birds.'"

We started laughing. It sounded exactly like something he would say.

After the plans were made, I spent the rest of the day in the hotel's hospitality room. Family members and friends continued arriving. I saw a small, dark-haired woman walking down the hallway toward me. It was Lisa, my best friend from SMU. My face lit up and I could feel my mouth moving slowly but firmly into a large smile. I had not seen her since the birth of her first son, nine years ago. She put her arms around me, and it was as if no time had passed. Our friendship had been maintained through Christmas cards and occasional phone calls.

Lisa was raised Catholic, but converted to Islam when she married her Pakistani husband. She now taught English at a Muslim school. After a brief exchange about her sons, my daughters, and life in general, we turned the conversation to recent events. "Deena, you know this isn't normal," said Lisa. "You know this is not a Muslim or Islam practice."

I told her I knew the difference.

Then she told me about how different her life was since 9/11. The school where she taught had received a bomb scare. Everyone had to be evacuated. It made me ashamed that someone would go to the trouble of frightening innocent people because they mentally couldn't separate the Muslim extremists from the rest.

After my conversation with Lisa, I wanted to be alone. I realized that I had not given enough thought to the long-term impact of 9/11. I was still only thinking of my own situation. Anything outside of my home and my family could only trickle in like single drops of water. This was another drop. And just like that, these drops were beginning to pool into a sense of responsibility to turn everything that had happened on September 11 – this incredible loss, the incredible pain I was experiencing – into something positive.

Suddenly awake from what seemed like a walking sleep, I thought about the different events in my life and in Tom's. Then our lives together. Everything was adding up to this moment. If the sum of all parts make the whole, then the path Tom and I had walked together and that I now walked alone was by design. Tom and I had talked many times how we believed God was calling us to do something more, something greater than what we had been doing. Maybe this was it.

Day by day I was pondering the varied pieces of the puzzle as they presented themselves. Gradually the fragments of a new goal were beginning to fit together and take on a more definite form in my mind. I would begin with the example I needed to set for my children, the message they needed to know about their father. If anyone else ended up benefiting, then it would be by God's grace. Halley, Madison, and Anna Clare. These precious gifts from God were my priorities.

Tom's convictions and what he stood for, how he lived his life, and the things he taught me, how my life changed knowing him, and what a positive impact he had on everyone's life who knew him, again I was reminded that the girls needed to know who he was. They would learn as I shared his message with the world. For my part, though, perhaps it was my calling not just to be his biggest admirer, but to carry forward the principles of goodness that had been his.

When Monday morning came, I was up before dawn with no worries about the memorial service. My only concern was for the children. I couldn't decide whether to keep them at home or let them attend a second memorial service. The first one had been difficult enough. On the other hand, I rationalized, there wouldn't be a body. Our families would be there to hold and comfort them, and years later I may regret them not going. I decided they should go.

St. Edward's church was only two blocks away from the Burnett home. As we approached the church, I saw hundreds of people standing outside dressed in red, white, and blue, holding flags, banners, and candles. Luminaries were placed on the sidewalks surrounding the church. The banners read, "Thank You Tom Burnett, American Hero," and "God Rest His Soul." Others waved, "We Love You Tom," and "U.S.A." The outpouring of love and compassion took my breath away.

The press was also there. Television cameras panned the children and me walking up the steps. Before entering the front doors, I was surprised to see several people from Thoratec to my left, including

Keith. I was glad to see them and stopped to say hello. Keith had a concerned look, similar to the one at the California memorial service.

"Hi Deena, how are you doing?" he asked.

"I'm doing OK," I said with a smile.

"No, really," he pressed. "What can I do for you? Do you want to go inside and sit down? You don't have to stand here and greet all these people. You know that, right? You can go inside and sit down."

"Really, I'm fine. I want to be here."

"Okay," he replied, concern still in his voice. "Deena, you better keep moving," he said, as a wave of people came through the door. I turned my attention to the rest of the Thoratec employees. There was Julie who had been in Paris on 9/11, Charles who lived in England, and Mike from Ohio. Tom would be humbled to know these particular people were here to pay their respects. They each had gone to great lengths to attend. I hugged each of them and thanked them for being there.

I gathered the girls, who so far hadn't realized why we were at church, and went inside. The auditorium was packed. People were everywhere, sitting and standing close together, overflowing into the aisles and the foyer. In fact, there was barely enough room to walk down the aisle. With each step, heads turned toward us. Their faces were sad. Their eyes were filled with tears. I had thought we were having a small private service. That's not what it had become, but it was okay.

With flowers decorating the altar and the American flag draped over Tom's picture as the backdrop, Monsignor Joe opened the service by saying, "What a difference a day makes."

The words resonated deep within me. What a difference a day makes. I briefly thought about what my life was like the day before September 11 and how different it was today. Then I turned to Mrs. Bev, who was sitting on my right, and I found myself more concerned about her than anyone else in the room. Would she make it through the service without completely breaking down? My pain was great, having lost a husband. How great hers must be having lost a son?

This was a much different service than the one in California. St. Isidore's was filled with strangers who had never known Tom. St. Edward's was filled with people who not only knew Tom, but loved him dearly. That love showed in the delivery of the spoken word: the Scriptures, the eulogies, and the Monsignor's stories.

When the service was over, I went to the reception hall to greet people. Many of Tom's high school and college friends, some of whom I had met before and others whom I had only heard about, were the first to introduce themselves. Many of them now lived on the East and West Coasts. But today, they left their wives at home to care for their children, and they traveled at great personal inconvenience to offer their respect to their dear friend. Forming a half circle around me, they all had the same look Keith did earlier. I could tell they wanted to say something, but weren't sure how to begin. Then finally one of them spoke.

"Deena, we want you to know that whatever you need, now or in the future, all you need to do is to let us know. Even though this group is small, we have incredible resources. Anything you need, anything, we can take care of it."

As I stood there, having heard every single word, I wondered what Tom would think of this? These were good people. They meant what they said, and I knew the girls and I didn't have anything to worry about. Tom had done the right thing and now God would put people and circumstances into our lives who would do the right thing for us – if and when we needed it.

The past few days had been days of putting one foot in front of the other to begin moving forward. And in return I had begun receiving small bits of comfort to hold onto and carry with me in the process.

I was struck by how normal life looked for everyone but me just one week after the attacks of September 11. Airports were open, commute traffic was flowing, schools were conducting classes, and homes were being managed. My life had come to a grinding halt and exploded into a media frenzy. The great pressing down of grief made it tempting to succumb to the depression which kept trying to dominate my mind. But instead, for the sake of our children, it was time to force myself to take even more deliberate steps to find the new normalcy in our lives that God intended. It would encompass much of what our lives had contained before and be broadened to include inspiring our girls and the world to live lives like Tom Burnett – lives which make a difference.

Chapter Nine

Finding A New Normal

"Death causes life as it was before with the individual to completely end, and the survivor must decide to find a new normal or a new beginning or a new state." – Carole Tarr

The next day I checked my messages. Mary had set up a voice mail system for me so I could more easily retrieve them from Minnesota. I had 60 that morning, and one of them was from the White House. I couldn't imagine why the White House would be calling.

I had forgotten that on Sunday, someone told me that Vice President Cheney had mentioned on *Meet the Press* that he was trying to reach me. Since I am somewhat skeptical and hadn't been watching television, I didn't know whether or not to believe it.

"Listen," I told my friends, "I've been on television and in the newspapers every day for a week. Dick Cheney used to be head of the CIA, he is the Vice President of the United States, and is one of the most powerful men in the world. If he can't find me, then this country is in bigger trouble than we think."

Everyone howled and laughed when I finished. And I enjoyed it. So when I heard the message from the White House, I really thought someone was playing a joke on me. I returned it anyway just to see what was going on.

"There are a whole lot of people in Washington who want to shake your hand, Mrs. Burnett," said a polished male's voice on the other end. He introduced himself as Ken Mehlman, a Senior White House

Advisor. "We want to know if you can come to Washington. How about tomorrow? Thursday? Or, what about Monday?"

If I could come on Thursday, then I was invited to attend the Presidential Address to Congress and the Nation scheduled for that evening.

"I'm afraid I can't come tomorrow," I said. "I don't want to leave my children, I have three daughters." He said he understood and they were welcome to come. He was certain he could find a babysitter once we arrived in D.C. Having them stay with a stranger didn't appeal to me, so I turned him down and said I could be there Monday. It would give me time to make arrangements for all of us to go: daughters, a babysitter, and Tom's family.

There was an uncomfortable pause. I could tell he was a little surprised that I wouldn't be there for such an important presidential speech. He wished me well and said he looked forward to meeting me some day.

Instead, I went to a birthday party that night for a friend. While I didn't particularly feel like going, I thought it might be good for the children: something fun.

But for me it was a mistake. It became difficult for me to sit around the kitchen eating pizza and birthday cake, talking about things that seemed so unimportant. I felt depression trying to set in.

I was reminded again how different my life now was. Sitting before me was this young couple who were happy and living in a beautiful home in a wonderful neighborhood. Everything was perfect for them. They had all of their goals and dreams ahead of them. All I could think was that my dreams had died on Flight 93. It wasn't their fault, but the smiling faces were beginning to smother me. I needed new goals and they needed to be goals of substance. The toast Tom used to make when drinking champagne kept running through my head:

"Live every day as though it were your last, for surely one day you will be right."

The White House called back on Thursday. It was Mr. Mehlman again. "I just wanted to ask you if you would be offended if Mrs. Beamer attended the Presidential Address to Congress and the Nation?"

I said, confused. "Why would I be offended?"

"I just wanted to check because we gave her a choice of coming today or Monday. We invited all three of you... Mrs. Glick, Mrs. Beamer, and you... but she was the only one who could come."

I didn't know who she was. I assumed she was someone's mother. "No, I don't mind." I said.

"Oh, okay. Well, thank you. Good-bye."

That night, the Burnetts and I watched the President give his special Address to Congress and the Nation. We were curious as to what he had to say about how our country was going to respond to the terrorist attacks.

I remembered a conversation Tom and I had once, when George W. first announced his campaign for the presidency. We were watching TV and one of the network anchors was going over Bush's background, referencing his past drinking problem, his poor grades, and other troubles in his youth. Then the anchor started talking about his presidential campaign. I turned to Tom and said, "Well, what do you think? Is that a guy you'd vote for?"

Tom didn't answer me right away. Then he said, "He'll have my vote."

I was quite surprised. Normally Tom would have supported a candidate who was much more articulate and thoughtful. At that time George W. Bush didn't give that impression.

"Don't worry," Tom continued. "Bush has the same resources Ronald Reagan had and that his father had. Don't worry about George W. Bush. He'll come into his own."

As the Burnetts and I listened to the President speak, I found it ironic that just two weeks prior this man had been struggling to define his presidency. It was clear to me now that this President had come into his own, on the day my husband died. I looked forward to meeting this man because I knew he was going to do great things.

When our entourage of the girls, the Burnetts, our friends, and I arrived at Reagan National Airport in Washington, D.C., there was some confusion about who was supposed to pick us up. Two different car services were waiting. In the commotion, a United Airlines representative said, "Ma'am, please come this way. And where's your husband? Are your husband and children with you?"

"My husband is dead," I said with a blank stare. It was the first time I said these words out loud.

His face went white with embarrassment. He didn't know what to say other than "I'm sorry." I blinked the tears away and asked which car was ours. As the driver took the bags, a lady pushing a stroller came towards me. With one arm reaching out, she quickly grabbed me and gave me a hug.

"I want you to know that my thoughts and prayers are with you," she said. She began to sob and walked off. This was the first time a stranger had recognized me. There was definitely a new normal for our lives.

The next morning the Burnetts and I had breakfast at the hotel. To my surprise, the restaurant was filled with other Flight 93 families. They all had the same haunted look that we had.

"I thought we were going to be the only ones," I said to Mr. Tom.

"Yeah, me too," he said.

A woman approached our table and introduced herself as Jeremy Glick's sister, Jennifer. By now I was vaguely familiar with some of the other names on board: Glick, Bingham, and Beamer. She told me Jeremy's wife, Liz, would be down in a few minutes and would want to meet me.

Over coffee, the Burnetts and I met Jeremy's family. As soon as Liz entered the room I recognized her. I had never seen her picture, but she had the same expression on her face as I did: blank, empty, tear-stained face with tired eyes. I immediately knew she had lost her husband, too. Without hesitating, I walked over and introduced myself. I had wanted to say more, but it was time to board a bus for the White House.

The White House looked exactly like I had seen it so many times on television. I never dreamed that my first visit to the White House would be under such trying circumstances. On any given day of my life, I would have been thrilled to be there. Not today.

It didn't feel right going to the White House without Tom. In the back of my mind, I always thought he could have been President of this country. Other people thought so, too. He had a comprehension of matters that went far beyond the average intelligence. He could look at situations, find results, and draw conclusions that no one else could see. Like everything Tom had done in his life, had he pursued a political career, I knew he would have been a successful.

Flag pins were handed out to the families. They had us sign some sort of waiver and the staffers told us no cameras were allowed. After we were ushered into the East Room, I began to feel incredibly sad. I hoped that what the President had to say would make me feel better.

The strain of their father's death and all the travel was wearing on the girls. While we waited, Anna Clare threw a temper tantrum. She wanted to sit on a bench that was on the other side of the room from me. Halley kept untying the ribbon on the back of her dress because it bothered her. It dragged on the floor when she walked. Madison was tugging at her tights constantly. She wanted them off. Instead of letting it upset me, I found myself comforted that they were behaving like children and it took my mind off the depressed mood for a few minutes.

As I glanced around the room at all the other families, I was looking for the widows, someone with whom I could identify. Then the President and First Lady came in, smiling. *How strange that they had such big smiles on their faces during such difficult circumstances.* Mrs. Bush in particular had the perkiest grin, and she looked very happy to be standing beside her husband. *What if your husband had been killed? How do you think you would have felt then?* On the other hand, I thought about how difficult it must be for her to try to relate to us when she couldn't possibly understand how we felt. I wondered if she was trying.

The President began to speak. Instead of being formal, he leaned forward with both elbows on the podium and seemed to take in all of us in the room. He talked about how everyone on the plane was a hero and that the nation was grateful, especially those who worked in the White House and the Capitol. He told us they would find out who was responsible and that they would be brought to justice. He seemed determined to get to the bottom of it all and took it personally that terrorism had attacked our country on his watch. He didn't try to make excuses for what happened, but said he would make sure it never happened again. While he may not have been able to understand our grief, he certainly understood the insecurity we were feeling, something the entire nation was feeling. Until his actions netted results, he was offering comfort the only way he could.

After he finished speaking, the President and Mrs. Bush went into the nearby Blue Room. Each family stood in line to meet them personally. We were among the last.

When it was finally our turn, I had each of the girls give a gift to the President and First Lady. Madison carried a 5x7 photo of Tom, Halley had a prayer card from the memorial service, and Anna Clare gave them a program. Handing him the photo, Madison looked at the President and said, "Did you know my daddy died?" She then dropped the photo, and the President bent down to pick it up.

"Yes, honey. I know your daddy died." Looking at the photo, he said, "Is this your daddy?"

"Yes."

"He sure is a handsome fella."

"Yes, he sure is," said Madison.

"What do we have here, are they triplets? No, twins?" asked the President.

"Yes. Halley and Madison are twins. Anna Clare is two years younger," I said.

"Twinsies," said the President.

"We have twin girls too," said the First Lady to Halley and Madison.

"Can they come out and play with us?" asked Madison.

The President and First Lady laughed.

"Our twins are older," said the President.

"Our girls are off at college," added the First Lady, "but if they were here, they would most certainly like to play with you."

With the girls learning there were no other kids to play with, they went off on their own to explore the room.

I shook hands with each of them. Each one placed their free hand on top of mine, and the President kissed me on the cheek.

"When the cockpit recordings are available, I would like to hear them," I said.

"I can see why you would want to," he answered. "They sure were heroes on that flight."

They both had tears in their eyes. I didn't mind anymore that the First Lady was smiling so much. Some people smile and laugh to hide the pain. Maybe that's what she was doing.

After each of us went through the receiving line, we stood for a photograph. Before we left, I turned to the President and said, "You know, my husband could very well have been President one day."

He smiled and said questioningly, "Oh?"

In a joking sort of way, I said, "I always told him I wanted to be First Lady."

"You would have been a good one," he said still smiling.

"I don't know. I'm afraid this is as close to the White House as I'm ever going to get."

"Well, you never know," he said.

I smiled with tears in my eyes. It was nice to have a lighter moment.

The same bus that brought us to the White House took us to the airport. I was still amazed at how thorough security was being with our luggage. Everything was searched by hand. It seemed like the Flight 93 families were singled out on every flight. *Of all people to suspect as being dangerous.* Then again, maybe they thought we would be easy targets. Or perhaps it was because Flight 93 didn't hit its target. Maybe we might be targets ourselves as retribution for what our loved ones did. The more I thought about it, the less I minded the inconvenience.

Near the gate, Anna Clare threw the biggest fit of her life. She was screaming her head off, yelling, "I hate you, Mommy. I hate you."

When I reached for her, she yelled, "Don't touch me! Get away from me!"

"It's okay, Anna Clare. I love you anyway," I said.

"Don't love me, Mommy. Don't love me," she said.

I couldn't win for losing. For the next 45 minutes, while we waited to board the plane, Anna Clare kept up her routine. My friend, Diane, became so embarrassed she wouldn't sit with us. I knew that today was the day an article about us was to appear in *People* magazine. Every newsstand in the airport would have it and who knows how many passengers might be reading it right at that moment, either on the plane or in the gate area.

I hope no one recognizes us. They're going to think I'm the worst mom in the world.

Once we boarded the plane, the flight attendants recognized us right away. They offered their condolences and asked if there was anything they could do to make our flight more comfortable. After sitting on the tarmac for almost an hour with Anna Clare sitting beside Diane, we headed back to the gate. *What's happening?* Then, as if reading my mind, one of the flight attendants came to me and said quietly, "I just want to let you know what's going on."

"Oh," I said, becoming alarmed. "What seems to be the problem?"

"There is a gentleman on board who is of Middle Eastern descent. So we're going back to the gate to let him off."

"Did he do something wrong?" I asked.

"No."

"Did he say something?"

"No, not that I know of."

"Why then do they want him off the plane?"

"Well, he looks like a typical business man to me, but just because he's of Middle Eastern descent, everyone is a little spooked. As you know, it's up to us whether a passenger stays or goes. I'm afraid this has been happening a lot lately."

Should I say something? It seemed like an injustice was being done to this man.

As he walked by with his briefcase in hand, he did indeed look like a typical businessman. But as badly as I wanted to say something, I didn't. I was afraid. I was afraid of who he might be and what he might do. *I have children on this plane.* I knew there must be reasons for his removal other than those she stated. I decided I didn't want him on board either.

Once he left the plane, I felt terrible. An incredible guilt washed over me. I should have stood up and said something. It wasn't right for me to assume. For a long, long time I regretted my decision.

We made it home very late that night, arriving an hour past midnight, and of course the girls' were up the next day at 7:00 a.m. I had planned on letting them stay home and sleep late. But if they were up, then they were going to school. Even though I was exhausted, it was good to be back home, especially since both memorial services were over. I was determined to get back into our daily routine and try to find our way through this maze of life without Tom.

At the children's school, I was stopped about every six feet by dozens of people who hugged me and cried, offering their condolences. I couldn't believe they actually knew me. We were new to the school that year. What an experience to have strangers walk up to me and know details about my life, like where and how I grew up, how I met my husband, and what he did for a living. They even knew how long we were married. All the details that normally take years to learn when getting to know someone, they knew before even meeting me.

As I stood, listening to them, watching them cry, my sense of security was strengthened by knowing the breadth of the compassion and support in my community. Especially since my family couldn't be there, it was nice to realize that people I didn't know yet, who knew me, were willing to help.

We started back with the girls activities as well. First on the list was Kumon, an after-school math and reading program. What had happened at their school repeated itself at the Kumon Center. Parents, who I had seen for almost two years but didn't know very well, talked to me as if we were old friends and reached out to offer help.

Next were Spanish classes. This was a new class they had not attended before. When I dropped them off, the girls didn't want me to leave. This was the first time they had showed any fear that they were worried something might happen to me. For some reason they were afraid if I left I wouldn't come back, so I waited outside the room for an hour. "If any of you become frightened, you can look right outside the window and I'll be here," I told them.

After class, they ran out and hugged me, holding on and not wanting to let go. Again, I reassured them. On the way home, Madison asked a question, which showed they had been thinking, "Mom, who will take care of us if something happens to you?"

In the pre-9/11 days, I would have said, "Your daddy will take care of you." Or, "you don't have to worry about anything because nothing is going to happen to me." But I couldn't say that anymore. I had two five-year-olds and a three-year-old who knew better. They knew that bad things do happen to good people. They knew that sometimes things happen and Mom and Dad can't come home.

"Let's come up with a plan," I said. Once home, I gathered everyone around the kitchen table and said, "How about we write down the names of every person who can take care of you if something happens to mommy?"

And so for the next half-hour, that's what we did. We made a long list of relatives in Minnesota and Arkansas. "There's Grandma and Grandpa and Daddy Mac and Granbe, "I started," and Mimi and Aunt Monica and Uncle Scotty and Aunt Martha and Uncle David and so on."

The list went on the refrigerator where everyone could see it. "If you ever get worried, you can just look at it and know there are lots of people who love you and are ready to take care of you," I said. It seemed to work.

But next day, on the way home from school, Madison added, "If something happens to you Mommy, who's going to take care of us until Grandma and Grandpa get here?"

I didn't have a ready answer, so that night we made another list. This time, it included neighbors. When we were done, Halley said, "But we don't know their phone numbers. How do we let them know when we need help?"

"Well, since they are our neighbors, you can just walk over and knock on the door," I said.

"But what if they're not home, mom?" said Madison. "Then what? How do we call them?"

I looked at the list on the refrigerator and suddenly realized there were no phone numbers. What's more, the girls didn't know how to read yet. So we color-coded each name with a corresponding number. Red was for Ms. Dena. Yellow was for Ms. Christine. Blue was for Ms. Erin. And so on. *That should do it.*

But before letting them go off to play, I told them there was one more important reason why they didn't have to worry. With their full attention, I said, "If anything happens to Mommy, God will know, and He will send someone to take care of you until Grandma and Grandpa get here."

It worked. In fact it worked a little too well. They started telling their friends at school about it, even complete strangers at the grocery store on occasion. "You know," Madison would say, "if your parents die and your brothers and sisters die, and all your aunts and uncles die, you don't have to worry because God will take care of you."

Whoever heard this must have thought my kids were evangelists. But I didn't mind. They had the right idea, so I let them talk. To know that God was always watching over them gave us peace of mind and a sense of security.

But just when I thought we were passed it all, Halley asked another question. "Mom, what street is our school on?"

"West El Pintado, but why do you want to know that?"

"Well, if you die on the way to school, I'll know where to tell the policeman to take us."

After all we had done, they were still afraid and wanted desperately to feel safe again. What more could I do?

That night we reviewed everything one more time. Afterwards, I told them there was one final thing we were going to do. "Girls, before leaving the house each morning, we're going to say a special prayer," I said. "It's called The Safety Prayer." Here is how it goes:

"Dear Heavenly Father, we come to you early this morning and we thank you for getting us through the night. We pray that you'll go with us throughout the day, hold our hands, guide us, and keep us safe. At the end of the day, bring us back home, safe and sound, so that we can be together. Amen."

The Safety Prayer became a daily ritual. The girls were so religious about saying it that they wouldn't go anywhere or do anything outside of the house without saying it in the morning. The Safety Prayer seemed to make all the difference. As prayer will do, it provided the final piece necessary for them to understand and take comfort in knowing that whatever happened God was walking with them.

As we adjusted to our new normal at home, my normal was expanding from that of a content housewife into something else. The White House wasn't the only political office reaching out. A number of politicians from California and Minnesota contacted me at both the state and federal level. They wrote and issued special letters of condolence and letters of proclamation, acknowledging my loss. They sent flowers, flags, and records from Congress and the Senate where Tom's actions had been noted.

Chapter Ten

Beginning the Fight for What Is True and Right

"A man does what he must – in spite of personal consequences, in spite of obstacles and dangers and pressures – and that is the basis of all human morality."
– John F. Kennedy (from Profiles in Courage)

On September 28, four days after meeting the President and First Lady, I visited with Congresswoman Ellen Tauscher of California. She was the first politician who wanted to visit me at my home.

Before she arrived, I found myself surprisingly calm. My hair was wet and in a ponytail. I was barefoot.

Mom had taken the children to the park and once I was alone, my mood quickly sank. With nothing to do but wait, I stood still at the front door, looking out and daydreaming of Tom.

When Congresswoman Tauscher arrived, she presented me with a flag that had flown in Tom's honor over the Capitol Building in Washington. We made our way into the living room and sat down. She proceeded to tell me how sorry she was that Tom had died and asked if there was anything she could do. "I work for you," she said. "Nothing is more important than whatever it is you need."

The first thing that came to mind was the cockpit recording. If she had any power at all, maybe she could help me.

"I want to hear the cockpit voice recorder," I told her. "I asked the FBI, but their response was that they would pass on my request. That was on September 11th. I've never heard back from them."

After hesitating a moment, she said, "You know it's going to be violent."

"Yes, I know."

The silence was noticeable.

"Maybe we should leave it up to the professionals to decide whether you should hear it," she said.

The word "professionals" made me uncomfortable. *What did she mean by that? Did she mean the FBI, politicians, or heaven forbid, doctors?*

"I believe anything having to do with my husband's death, I should know," I said sternly.

"Absolutely, I understand," she said, "And I'll do anything and everything I can to provide that for you."

Then she went to talk about the twists and turns my life might take over the next few weeks and months. "You know you'll probably be called on to do a number of things," she said. "The kind of things you've never done before."

What did she mean?

"And I must say, you're doing very well," she said. "We're all very proud of how strong you have been, but it's going to get worse before it gets better."

Who was "we"?

She sounded as if she was speaking from experience. She wrote down her phone numbers – home, cell, and pager – then said, "Call anytime."

She must have seen a look on my face that said, "I'm never going to call."

"Really," she insisted. "I want you to call. And if you come to Washington, I want you to stay with me."

Before she left, she hugged me with a very genuine embrace. I didn't think I would ever hear from her again. But I was wrong. I was surprised when her office called a week later to see how I was doing. They also wanted to let me know Tauscher was working on trying to get the cockpit recordings released to the families of Flight 93. They said she already had a meeting with the FBI, and that she sent a letter requesting the recordings be released. She even informed the press of her activities.

She did what she said she would do, and I was impressed by her integrity. It's rare to find someone who stands by their word. It's even more rare to find this in politics.

Her office also volunteered to help me in a number of other ways with administrative issues related to 9/11. Tauscher's office called every week for months just to see how we were doing.

At the end of September, I was contacted by another political office. California Governor Gray Davis called and wanted to know if I would speak at the California Day of Remembrance on October 9. Without hesitation, I agreed. This was the first time I had been asked to speak. The Governor's office said they expected over 10,000 people.

Nothing had changed in my feelings about public speaking. I was still nervous. At first I didn't know what I wanted to say. But one thing had become clear to me since September 11. I wanted everyone to know that not only did my husband and the people of Flight 93 die defending the freedom and privileges that we have today, but there were hundreds of thousands of others who preceded them in death protecting these very same rights.

I wanted people to really think about that. I wanted them to become aware that our freedom isn't free. It never has been. Prior to 9/11 my generation had never truly experienced the hardship of war. We were too young to feel any impact even from Vietnam. Except for a short period during the first Gulf War, we had never experienced the fright of having our brothers and fathers and uncles and neighbors shipped off to war with the possibility of not coming home.

I also wanted people to think about how they felt on the day of September 11 and acknowledge that our country's security had been compromised. I wanted them to know that these things happen in other countries every day with the populations at large living in fear of not knowing whether they are going to be safe when they leave their home.

Finally, I wanted them to think about why they had never had to experience that feeling before that dreadful day.

I began to make notes. I thought about the beginning of our country, our forefathers, and the Constitution. I pondered what it must have meant to these men who wrote it and then debated what should go into the laws that have since been the foundation of our democracy. I also thought about the Pilgrims. What must they have seen when they first landed? How did they feel seeing the shores of our country for the first time? What did they think of its beauty? How different everything must have looked from their homeland. I thought about the books my husband had read and shared with me on the Civil War and World Wars I and II. He had been amazed at the courage and valor of the men who fought in those wars. Many of them had marched into battle, knowing they would die, and yet for the price of freedom they gave up their lives willingly. The freedom for which they fought was something they passed on to their children.

All these emotions I poured out on paper. The culmination of a lifetime of loving America, my years of marriage to good citizen Tom, and the bittersweet significance our pledge of allegiance and flag now held for me. I hoped that I would express myself in a way that would move others to be inspired by the same thoughts.

A few nights before I was supposed to give the speech on the steps of the California State Capitol in Sacramento, I e-mailed it to a few of my friends who were journalists, asking if they could offer suggestions. I felt my inexperience could only benefit from their experience. To my surprise, they all sent it back with the same message, "Don't change a thing."

Just to be safe, I took the speech with me to a friend's house for dinner.

After we ate, I showed the speech to my friend. When I asked for feedback, he said he liked it, but he had a friend whom he described as being the "smartest guy" he knew. He was a professor at the University of Chicago and my friend suggested I send him the speech.

When I returned home that night, I e-mailed it to him. The next day, we spoke on the phone. He was excellent at assisting me in more clearly expressing my thoughts. We rearranged some of the paragraphs for better flow, and he suggested I acknowledge the military.

I still wasn't traveling anywhere without my girls. So the day before the speech, I drove my mom, the children, and myself to a hotel in Sacramento, which lies about an hour and a half east of San Ramon. Over dinner at the hotel restaurant, a woman by the name of Deborah Borza introduced herself. "I know my daughter must have been thrilled to be on that flight with your husband," she said.

For a moment I was confused. Then I realized that just as it had been at the White House there were other Flight 93 families staying at the hotel. What an incredible tribute she had spoken about my husband! Especially when her daughter had died on that flight. Next Alice Hoglan, mother of Mark Bingham, approached me and said, "I want to tell you I am so grateful you were able to provide your husband with the information you did that morning." I had immediate respect for women who could emit such strength and grace to provide comfort to someone else when they were feeling so much pain themselves. I liked these women and I knew I would hold them dear forever. I only hoped I would have the opportunity to get to know them better.

The next morning, in an auditorium down the street from the Capitol Building, Governor Gray Davis addressed us. Following a five-minute speech, he made his way around the room to speak one-on-one with each family.

After everyone had their photograph taken with the Governor, we were all called out to make our way to the steps of the Capitol in parade-like fashion. The streets were lined on both sides with thousands of people waving American flags and clapping their hands, yelling "Thank You" and "God Bless America" and "Thank you for your sacrifice."

I walked beside Alice. There were crowds ranging from school children to Islamic groups reaching out to shake our hands. Alice was smiling and waving, and she said, "Deena, lift your hand, wave, and smile! These people want to see you. They want to say thank you. They are here to honor Mark and Tom, and everyone else on Flight 93."

This was so hard and yet it was so good. I may have been a housewife, who loved her quiet voice, but today I had been given a forum from which to speak forth my message and I was going to do it! I lifted my heavy hand into the air. As tears streamed down my face, I tried to force a smile. "Oh, I hope these people don't think I'm happy just because I'm trying to smile."

Deborah Borza was now walking with us. "Deena," she said, "I read the speech you're going to give today. I want you to know that you're right on the mark. You get up there, and you say it with strength. You say it with honor. Everyone here will be glad to hear those words."

We marched on and finally arrived at the platform above the State Capital steps. There we received instructions as to who would sit where, who would stand where, and how we were to receive the flags which had flown over the capitol once they were presented. Photographers crawled on their knees, trying to stay out of the way of the television cameras. News reporters came up to us with their notepads, asking our names, how to spell them, and whom we'd lost on Flight 93.

Looking around, I saw several chaplains sitting across the aisle from us. I was glad they were there. Deborah must have noticed the look of distress in my face for she said, "Deena, tell me what it is you need right now. Just whatever comes to your mind, tell me. I mean it. The first thing."

"What I need right now is for the grace of God to come over me."

She took both my hands, looked into my eyes, and said, "It's done."

With that, I took a deep breath, shook off my doubt, and let God take over. I had never spoken to thousands of people. For the first time that morning, by God's power I thought I might actually pull it off.

Then they called three names: Alice Hoglan, Paul Holm, and mine. I was glad there would be three of us up there.

Paul gave the first speech with Alice and me standing behind him. He didn't talk long and I was too nervous to remember much of what he said. When Paul finished, he stepped back and Alice stepped forward. She confronted the despicable acts of the terrorists, calling them cowards for killing innocent victims, then hiding. Then she gave one quote I will never forget: "Bravery is not the absence of fear, but the courage to act in spite of it." When she stepped back from the microphone it was my turn.

I took a step toward the podium and thought I was going to be ill. *How am I going to do this?* As I lay the papers down, a great calm came over me. *God's Presence.* I looked into the sea of faces before me, and it seemed as if not a single person was moving. The wind had stopped blowing and every tree stood still. Everyone and everything was as if waiting.

I began to speak slowly at first, in a soft still-unsure voice. Then, with each word, I heard myself grow louder and stronger. I was no longer reading the speech, but rather I was delivering it with the same kind of emotion it had evoked in me when I wrote it.

"We're going to do something." Those were the last words my husband said to me from Flight 93. Although I never heard from him again, his actions are well known.

He and his fellow passengers were the first to ever fight back against terrorism. They gathered information, assessed the situation, and in the tradition of our great nation voted to change their destiny. They rose from their seats and did something. As a result, we believe thousands of lives were saved and our federal government buildings are still standing.

This is not the first time a small group of people has changed the course of history. In 1620 men and women walked off a ship and built a colony at Plymouth Rock. This was the beginning of our country, and they became a symbol of courage and faith.

Years later, another small group of people sat in a room in Philadelphia and drafted an unprecedented document – the Constitution – outlining the principles of our freedom.

Over the years, it has been common citizens – neighbors, friends, families – who have been willing to rise from their seats and do something to preserve and protect the freedom this document offers – often at the expense of their own lives. The events that shook our nation on September 11 are a reminder that the defense of our freedom is never done.

Tom often spoke of the importance of being a good citizen. He was a true patriot. He loved our country and was concerned about the moral direction in which we were headed. He had a keen sense of right and wrong. He believed good values and high morals were not debatable. Most importantly, he practiced what he preached.

Tom taught me a toast not long after we were married. He would raise his glass and say, "Live every day as if it were your last, for surely one day you will be right."

If this were your last day on earth, ask yourself: "What have I done to make a difference? Is the life I lead worth someone else dying for?"

It's not an idle question. Many have died for our freedom. Even now, the men and women of our armed forces are in harm's way and some may not return to their homes and families. The majority of us here will never be called upon to defend our nation with our lives, but each of us should live a life worthy of those who have.

Those who have selflessly given the last full measure of sacrifice deserve no less from us than this pledge:

"We will find out the needs of our community and we will meet them. We will rise from our seats and do something!"

Take action every day. Help your neighbor. Volunteer in your schools and community. Vote. Support our President. Go to church, have faith and pray. LOVE YOUR FAMILY. Teach your children to respect the freedom that so many men and women have lost their lives defending. In short, be a good citizen!

Citizenship and valor can be found in deeds both large and small – as small as being kind to one another and as large as laying down your life for those around you.

Tom's telephone call to me is now a call to us all. In the spirit of my husband and the passengers of Flight 93, I challenge you to get up and do something positive.

In the words of Margaret Meade, "Never doubt that a small group of people can change the world, indeed it is the only thing that ever has."

When it was over, I returned to Alice's side. To my left, I noticed Governor Davis moving toward me. He embraced me and said, "That was a wonderful, wonderful speech Deena. Thank you."

After he let go, I looked at one of the chaplains, who winked at me and smiled.

"Was that okay?" I asked.

"That was more than okay," she said. "Look."

I glanced at the crowd. Everyone was standing and cheering. *I must have done all right.* So I sat down and took off my jacket. Even though it was terribly hot, I was frozen in my chair.

Several State Senators and Representatives approached. I didn't realize there were so many dignitaries seated in my section. Everyone shook my hand and offered their thanks for the sacrifice I was enduring and said they were grateful for the words I had chosen to speak.

When the chaplains drew near, they asked how I was holding up. Trying to keep from breaking down, I said to one of them, "Could you pray for me?" Three of them gathered around, laid their hands on me, and began to pray. When they finished, I thanked them. We went back to the hotel in procession. Along the route, strangers came up to me on every side to shake my hand. One little girl asked for my autograph. I was dumbfounded. "You want my autograph?" I said. She nodded and said yes. As I signed her paper, I still couldn't believe that she wanted my autograph. Didn't she know I was nobody special?

A woman whose son had died on Flight 93 approached and said, "Deena, you said what we wanted to say but couldn't find the words. Thank you." Another woman, who I met briefly the previous night, whose parents were on board the plane that hit the Pentagon, hugged me and said, "We find the strength we didn't know we had. And when you need it, it's always there. I see that in you. Thank you." Then she walked away.

When I was near the hotel, a man dressed in a fireman's uniform stopped me. "I want you to know how moved I was by the speech you gave today," he said.

"Thank you," I replied.

"I guess I just really wanted to make a connection with someone who was here, and I feel like I'm being led to make that connection with you. I don't know why. I can't explain it. But I would really like to get to know you better given the opportunity."

I looked deep into his eyes, trying to figure out what was on his mind. He seemed deeply wounded by what happened on September 11. He offered me his card and asked for my address. He wanted to write me a letter. I wrote it down. It seemed like he wanted to talk longer, but I had been away from my children for nearly two hours. I had to get back to them and make sure they were safe. I thanked him and went on my way. (Later on, he did write.)

I considered where I had come since September 11, less than a month before. Certainly my grief was no less. But where Tom had done the right thing, I wanted to also. I was beginning to find my way, the new way I was supposed to go. I was working to get the girls' lives back to a semblance of normal. And I had taken my first big step today to step out and deliver the message which was part of Tom's legacy. My steps had no joy in them yet, but they were deliberate and purposeful. It was a start. Yes, it had been a hard day. But it had been good.

Chapter Eleven

Persevering Through Darkness Until Dawn

I will lead the blind by ways they have not known, along unfamiliar paths I will guide them; I will turn the darkness into light before them and make the rough places smooth.
– The Bible, Isaiah 42:16

It was the second week of October, and we were back in San Ramon. On Friday morning, Halley's kindergarten class opened Chapel at school. The kids were supposed to go on stage and sing songs about Jesus and recite biblical verses and poems. Though this was the school's first activity attended by parents, I didn't think it would bother me that Tom wasn't there. Even if he had been alive, Tom wouldn't have been able to attend. His job always had demanded the majority of his time during the week.

When I arrived, everything was true to my expectations. What a relief. Halley was absolutely darling on stage, waving and smiling as she sang. Yet I had mixed feelings. While I was happy for her, I was sad for Tom. This would be the first of many activities he would miss.

My heart was still unbearably heavy. One holiday after the next loomed on the horizon. I was depressed most of the time, fighting the urge to climb into my bed and stay there even though I knew I couldn't. Truly, I was making every effort to participate in things as I normally would. But everything took such an effort and there was no joy, just putting one foot in front of the other in order to be a mother to my daughters. Yet with that, I reminded myself that I was "doing something."

That weekend, I took the girls to the pumpkin patch. We were gearing up for Halloween. The kids called it a Halloween Adventure.

We walked around the pumpkin patch and picked out possible jack-o-lanterns. Everything we did that day was a reminder Tom was missing. A year ago we had done the exact same things in the exact same places, but Tom had been with us. He had taught all of us – even me – how to carve our first jack-o-lanterns. This year, the girls looked to me to carve out a face. I wasn't sure if I knew how, but I would figure it out. I was not going to disappoint them.

Back home, the girls were anxious to pull out the Halloween decorations from boxes in the garage. We had bought them back in August when they first appeared in stores. In years past, we had always used cute decorations like scarecrows and happy-faced pumpkins. But this year the children, still carefree in August when we shopped, had selected decorations with a focus on "scary." Standing in the garage surrounded by all the skeletons, skulls, and tombstones, I felt a spirit of death closing in around me. For the first time, I thought Halloween was a morbid holiday. I put away all the symbols which portrayed life as if it ended in ashes and resurrected our old cute decorations which emphasized harvest and the beauty of autumn instead. Additionally, if we were going trick-or-treating this year, we would do it in a fun way instead of one which reminded us of death. The girls were thrilled with the idea of dressing up as princesses.

I looked at my calendar. October 31st was just a week away and I was reminded that Laurie Hart was coming over. Her husband, John, had died in the World Trade Center on September 11th when he had gone back in to help someone else. I was really looking forward to meeting her. It would be great having someone around who understood firsthand what I was experiencing.

I learned an important lesson through her visit. For me, it was still too early to do a lot of sharing. While I could share a little, it was dangerous for me to be in conversations which caused me to sense the intense pain of others. She had four children. Like me, she had a sad story. She seemed lost to the point that I wanted to help her but I knew I couldn't. I was not strong enough to carry my own pain, let alone to emotionally take on the loss of another. It was too easy for me to be pulled down deeper into the cesspool of depression. I was fighting with all my might to keep my head up and crawl out. It was comforting to know I was not alone, but when she left, I thought it best that we not get together too often. It seemed emotionally draining for both of us.

Halloween was finally upon us. Before Tom died it always had been such a fun family night out for us. We both took the girls trick-or-treating, and Tom would try to capture everything on video camera. In the videos you could hear him trying to get the girls to speak into the camera, "What kind of candy did you get? Make sure to say thank you. Take turns ringing the doorbell. Whose house should we go to now?"

I ached in his absence. To make the holiday bearable, friends had invited us over for the evening. The husbands took the kids trick-or-treating, and the women stayed behind. Halley, Madison, and Anna Clare did much better than I. We didn't stay long after they returned with their sweet treasures. I needed to get home.

On the way I thought about how we had struggled to make it through each day of October – the first full month on our own. But we had done it! This gave me hope. We could get through November, too.

It was All Soul's Day. I had been asked by Father Frank to present the gifts of bread and wine at Mass in celebration of Tom's life. I was honored to do so, but this time I left the girls with a babysitter.

When I arrived at St. Isidore's, a woman approached and introduced herself as June. Her husband had been killed in January 2001 when he had been hit by a drunk driver while bicycling. When she extended her hand to say hello, I was struck by the emptiness in her eyes. An alarm in me went off. I recognized that look. It stared back at me every time I saw my reflection in the mirror. I was horrified. Her husband had died almost 11 months ago and the haunted, lost look was still there. My heart sank. How long was this emptiness inside me going to last? I could not bear the thought of it being almost a year.

It had not even been two months and I was tired of it. I just wasn't an unhappy person. In fact, throughout my entire life, I always had been the exact opposite. I was the kind of person who found joy in little things – from planting flowers in the backyard to taking the kids on Saturday morning walks in the park. My joy had always been making others happy. When we moved into a new community, it was I who went around and introduced myself to all the neighbors. When others moved in, it was I who was first at their front door with a welcoming face. I organized neighborhood playgroups. I even planned social activities throughout the year, so people in the neighborhood could meet one another.

Now, even though I had more friends in my life than ever before, I couldn't seem to enjoy them. All I thought about was Tom not being here. His absence seemed to prevent me from taking pleasure in anything. It was becoming imperative to find more ways to channel my grief into something positive, something that would help me turn this tragedy into something good, if not for myself and my family, then at least for someone else. I longed to replace the emptiness in me with the fullness of something meaningful.

I knew many, many people had been impacted by Tom's heroic actions. The countless letters and phone calls I had received since September 11 made this clear. I knew part of my job was to get the message out that we all needed to do the right thing, become better citizens, and do something. Despite my initial nervousness, I had begun taking the message before more audiences as I was invited to speak at additional events. I was encouraged when one woman even said, "Deena, I feel from you not just an ability to affect people, but also to transform them."

The speech I had given at the State Capitol on October 9th continued to have positive ripple effect. I had heard that the text of the speech had been circulated to small-town newspapers and had been printed in some church bulletins. I had been told by many that what I had expressed were the very things others wanted to say, but lacked the words. (Later I learned that my speech was even read aloud at some family Thanksgiving dinner tables that year.) So the message I needed to deliver was beginning to congeal and have an effect beyond me. But I felt that these one hundred or so words were not enough.

People were responding to the idea of promoting a stronger value system in America as a living memorial to those who died. My sense of responsibility to them was growing. I wanted to help in their grief and healing. I wanted to give them a source of light into our lives and the life Tom led. I wanted everyone to learn from his experiences and to recognize the importance of living by your convictions: knowing the difference – really knowing the difference – between right and wrong, and choosing to do what is right even when faced with the potential of death.

I prayed to the Lord for guidance. If this was the message God wanted me to deliver, then I would do it. But He would have to give me the strength, the words and the opportunity for this was not my talent.

June and I spoke after Mass. I learned she had turned the pain of her sorrow into the positive power of activism by getting involved in Mothers Against Drunk Driving. She went to schools and lectured about the importance of not drinking. She felt like she had found a sense of purpose in her husband's death when she could share with others how to live a better way. It was clear the death of her husband changed her life in a way similar to how mine seemed to be changing. There was simply a need to take the intensity of emotion and re-direct it to make a tangible, positive impact on the lives of others.

June's purpose was to fight against drunk driving. My message concerned sharing Tom's story in such a way that his example would empower individuals to become good citizens who are not afraid to do what needs to be done. I wanted to encourage them to go back to church and put honoring God as the center of their lives so that the fruit of higher morals and better values would be produced across our land.

Tom and I both believed our country had been moving in a direction opposite to this for some time. Since Tom was a man who had lived and died by his convictions, this opened the way for me to use his life and actions as an example to help turn others in the right direction. If people paid attention to what Tom had done, maybe they would start to think about why he did it. If people sought to mirror his actions, perhaps they would begin to reflect his beliefs and gain his sense of right and wrong. Over time it was possible more and more people might develop the strong foundation within themselves from which right action and courage spring forth.

November was the Alumni Awards Dinner to be held at Pepperdine University in Malibu, California where Tom had earned his Master's degree in business administration. I was to attend the event in order to accept the Distinguished Alumni Award on his behalf. Since we were long overdue for a family vacation, I took Mom and the girls and arrived a few days early.

We stayed at a lovely beach house owned by Pepperdine. There we were secluded so no media could find us. It was the first time I had been able to relax since 9/11. We fed the sea gulls and walked along the beach in our bare feet. The girls roasted marshmallows in the fireplace.

The night of the alumni dinner, Keith, who was also a Pepperdine alum, was my escort. We were supposed to meet during the cocktail hour and then go into the ballroom. While I waited, many people approached, introducing themselves and expressing their condolences. One gentleman pursued such a random, off-the-wall conversation with me that I literally laughed out loud. My laughter surprised me. It felt so good to have the heaviness lift for a moment. Perhaps I was getting better.

The ballroom was vast with huge video screens on each side. The tables were draped with purple silk and gold fabric. Enormous floral arrangements were used as centerpieces. It was a positive "do something" evening. I accepted the award on Tom's behalf and helped launch a scholarship in his name for the Graziadio Business School. Pepperdine University then presented me with three full-tuition scholarships for Halley, Madison, and Anna Clare. I was astonished and grateful. What a wonderful evening! I was glad I went.

In mid-November the girls, Mom, and I attended a tree-lighting ceremony at the Hyatt Regency in downtown San Francisco. The hotel was known for having the largest hotel lobby in the world. Every year, they had an enormous Christmas tree, which usually was lit by a celebrity. This year they had asked me.

I thought it would be fun for the children to see the decorations and be a part of something festive. It was our first opportunity to do something fun and lighthearted in a public venue. Together we flipped the switch that lit the tree. The girls were enamored with the beautiful bright lights. Later that night, we sat on the balcony of our hotel room and watched fireworks shoot into the sky as ice skaters dressed in Christmas attire performed below. When Santa skated out onto the ice with all the little elves, the kids screamed with excitement. It breathed life into me to hear their unabashed joy. I couldn't have asked for a better way to start the holidays.

Yet I was not looking forward to Christmas. Thanksgiving was only a week away. The children were excited about both holidays, and I had avoided thinking about them. Tomorrow, we were supposed to be on a plane to Minnesota to spend Thanksgiving with the Burnetts. I hoped the kids' excitement would enliven my spirit.

Thanksgiving with the Burnetts wasn't something I could cancel even if I wanted to. Tom's youngest sister Mary Margaret was getting married the Saturday after. Tom had bought our plane tickets early in the summer.

Unlike the previous plane ride, this one went smoothly. The passage of time was wielding its healing power. When we landed, the entire Burnett family was there to greet us. It was great seeing them again. It was going to be a busy time with the bridal luncheon, a parade of visitors, errands to run, hair appointments, etc.

Mid-week, I decided to take the girls shopping for a wedding gift. It was the first time I had been to a mall since September 11. The possibility of shopping malls being a target of terrorist attacks had kept me away.

There were hardly any people there. While it made for no line to have our annual visit with Santa Claus, it reminded me of again of how 9/11 had affected the whole country. Shopping for Mary's gift, I tried to think what Tom might want to give to her. But it hurt too much, so I chose something on her registry and left.

The family had decided it would be best if we did something different for Thanksgiving. Rather than spend the holiday gathered around the Burnetts' dining room table, we had made a reservation for 20 at the country club.

The buffet-style dinner was beautifully apportioned and delicious. But the mood at our table was somber and quiet. There was no getting around it. It was a tough day. Everyone tried to smile, but there was little conversation.

Despite our best efforts, Tom was on all of our minds. I sat next to Mr. Tom. There wasn't any of the usual Thanksgiving light-heartedness. No one cracked jokes about the family gravy boat. No political discussions or heated debates. We just sat there trying to eat our food, using attention on the children as an occasional reason to break the silence. "Halley, have you had enough to eat?" "Madison, don't you like sweet potatoes?" "Do you need another beverage, Anna Clare?" I snuck sidelong glances periodically at Mr. Tom to see how he was holding up. The tears in his eyes were my answer.

The next day our focus turned to Mary's wedding. There were eight of us at the Macaroni Grill for the bridal luncheon. It was only family and prospective family. This was to be Mary's special time. We went out of our way not to mention Tom or September 11 and to keep our attention on Mary. But it seemed that everyone was worried about me. Often there was an awkward pause as the others waited for my reaction to comments before reacting with their own smiles or tears. It was like everyone was on eggshells around me. Meanwhile, I was trying to focus on Mary, trying to be happy for her. I didn't want my sadness to spoil her happiness.

There were the usual bridal games to play. Each of us shared our own words of wisdom with Mary on life and marriage. We compiled them in the form of a diary. As we sat there, tasked with writing down 10 things we knew for certain about life, the process made everyone cry except me. Instead my tears flowed when it came time to read what I had written out loud:

1. The sun always rises
2. Nothing is for certain
3. Little things don't matter
4. Little things always matter
5. Good credit and good education are two necessities you'll never regret having
6. God is in heaven
7. We all grow older
8. Each moment will soon be a moment past
9. There will be more good moments than bad if you so choose
10. Life is never long enough

Then, I shared three things I held to be true about marriage. First, it is more fun to wake up together than alone. Two, children change everything. Three, in 20 years, it is not your love that keeps you together, but your commitment to your marriage.

As I finished I was struck by the irony of giving marital advice when I was no longer married.

Mary originally had planned on having a traditional Catholic ceremony with about 200 people. But after September 11, she decided to scale it back dramatically and have only immediate family – about 20 people total. There were so few of us that we were each given a part in the wedding. Halley, Madison, and Anna Clare were to be flower girls. I was to read a scripture verse.

The next day at the wedding, they were dressed beautifully in their long flowing satin dresses with tulle skirts. Halley was first down the aisle. She handed tiny peonies to each of the ladies sitting at the ends of the pews. Next came Anna Clare. Halfway down the aisle, she became embarrassed. Turning abruptly, she ran back up the aisle smack into

Madison. The two of them fell to the floor, peonies flying through the air. I was absolutely horrified. They came to their feet, kissed, and went down the aisle together. Everyone began to laugh, including the bride. It actually provided exactly the bit of humor the day needed.

The reception was held in a private room at the country club. It was splendidly beautiful and perfect.

We all wanted the night to be perfect for Mary and I think we did a good job leaving our sadness behind for one night. But every once in a while, little things like a loving look exchanged between the bride and groom, the children playing in the corner, or a special song triggered memories of my own wedding. I left the room twice that night, hoping no one would notice. I would excuse myself to the ladies lounge, cry, wash my face, apply powder and lipstick, then reenter the ballroom smiling and ready to chat.

I didn't just love Tom, I adored him. I loved him so much that the love I had for him carried through into everything I did. When that love was ripped away, a hole was created that could never be filled again. Even though I was genuinely happy for Mary, that happiness didn't nullify my own sadness and pain.

At the end of the evening, we watched a video about the bride and groom growing up through the years. Many of Mary's photographs included pictures of Tom. It was the first time any of us had seen so many photos of Tom since he died. No one could hold back their tears. We cried unabashedly together.

I was glad the wedding was over. It had been much harder to endure than Thanksgiving. I loved the Burnetts, but I was looking forward to going home.

With only four days left in November, Congresswoman Tauscher's office called. She had just sent a formal letter on my behalf to FBI Director Robert Mueller, requesting that the cockpit recordings be released to the family members. They also said she had made a statement to the media late Monday saying she was officially working on my behalf.

The San Francisco Chronicle broke the news Tuesday morning. Blindsiding me, the media was at my doorstep tenfold. They wanted to build a story around my efforts to listen to the cockpit recording where they could malign the FBI for being unresponsive and insensitive toward a 9/11 widow. They wanted me to help to make the story.

I knew they were trying to make this into something greater than it was.The television program *20/20* sent a producer to my house. *Good Morning America* called. Everyone wanted to know if I would fly to Washington to confront the FBI, and if so, could they get an exclusive. I disappointed everyone by telling them it wasn't that big of a deal. I had made a simple request and everything was proceeding as it should. "I am confident the recordings will be released," I said.

The media wasn't very happy with my patience. They wanted something more dramatic. I told them I had nothing more to say. I wasn't going to turn a non-issue into a media sensation. They eventually left me alone, but not before they had stirred the nest at the FBI.

The following day I received a heated call from the Director of the FBI Office in San Francisco wanting to know exactly what was going on. His agency was being portrayed poorly in the news. It was reported that I had made several phone calls to his office and left messages that weren't being returned. He wanted to know who had received my calls, with whom I had left messages, and with whom did I wish to speak. I tried to assure him that I was not upset. I told him that I had placed three phone calls during the first few weeks after September 11, none of which had been returned. Unfortunately, I hadn't written down the names of the people with whom I had spoken.

The conversation with the FBI instigated by the media attempting to blitz me again was more than I could handle. I had to do something, but I didn't know what. I wasn't about to let things get out of control. I called Keith. He would know what to do.

During the last few months, his friendship had been invaluable. He was level-headed, thoughtful, and always had a clear solution to problems. He had been vigilant since Tom's death in checking in with me and making sure my needs were met.

I looked forward to his visits and phone calls. He was the only person in the San Francisco Bay Area who knew Tom well. Time with Keith provided comfort that no one else could provide because he could say things about Tom that brought back memories which made me laugh instead of cry. No one else had known Tom well enough to do that. Talking with him had been a great way to work through some of the sadness I was feeling.

But I was becoming emotionally dependent on Keith. This wasn't good. If I was still depending on someone else, how was I ever going to get better? I needed to find my own way and not rely so heavily on someone else to guide me.

Besides, I was getting increasingly frustrated. Wherever I turned for help, the advice I received, no matter how well intended, just didn't seem to hit the mark. The books on grief I read were, for the most part, not helpful. When I talked with my friends, it was more like I was venting than working through concerns constructively. Keith was helpful, but only up to a certain point and maybe I had reached that point. It was my life – no one else's. Had the time come when I could be my own best help, I wondered?

I was determined to fight my way out of this depression. I remembered the first time I went deep sea fishing with Tom. He'd been skeptical. He thought I would get sea sick and ruin the trip. He assured me that if I was determined to go, I would have to practice the theory of "mind over matter." It seemed to work.

I was tired of being sad. I had been numb for so long. I refused to take medication. I wanted to feel the pain without it being masked by a pill. I felt I owed that to Tom. I had a reason to be sad, not a biological disorder. But now, perhaps I could use my mind to overcome the depression. Anytime I found myself laughing or feeling good about anything, I made myself become intensely aware of that emotion. I measured my emotional state of mind on an imaginary scale, gauging whether I was improving or getting worse.

I had to get better for the children. I wasn't spending enough time with them. They wanted more attention, needed more attention, and I wasn't giving it to them. I was distracted. The media demanded much of my time as did public appearances and giving speeches. Even though my schedule was better than it had been, I couldn't help but think the girls' behavior wasn't what it should be. They didn't seem happy. They weren't laughing like they used to. They were whiney and clingy. Anna Clare was angry all the time. They needed discipline.

In many ways, it seemed they were experiencing the same kind of emotions I was, but from a child's perspective. The difference was that being the adult, I was supposed to set the example. So far, I wasn't happy with the example I was setting.

I needed a new beginning. I needed to do something – the right thing. I couldn't control the fact that Tom was not there, but I could decide to make life as good as possible under the circumstances. Everyone told me to wait one year before making life-altering decisions. And yes, I understood the reasons behind the advice. But I could not allow anyone's advice to dictate which decisions I should make nor the timeframe in which to make them. I needed to stand on my own two feet instead of relying so heavily on others. I had to take responsibility for my own situation. I was 37 and had three children to raise. Hmmmm… I actually began to believe that I could do it.

I knew the next right thing to do. If I was ever to move forward and make a difference in the lives of many, I had to take care of us first. Our home had to be built on a solid foundation. Even though I felt a responsibility to everyone who wanted something from me, I put on the brakes and took steps to ensure that our home and the relationships between the girls and myself received the highest priority.

I learned to say no to all the people who were calling. My children's needs became the source of urgency for change. They made me re-consider my priorities and try to figure out a way to re-position us so that I was living the message I was preaching. I was telling others to make a difference in their lives, and yet I needed to make a difference in my own – beginning at home, by building a strong foundation with my own children.

At a time when incoming requests began to speed up, (the media wanted year-end stories for the holidays) I decided not to just slow it down, but to turn it off. No more interviews. No more appearances for now. I stopped returning their phone calls. I put an end to all unnecessary travel. It wasn't worth it anymore. It was taking too much time away from my children.

Within our home, I worked to re-establish routine. I focused on what needed to be done, not on what everyone else asked me to do. The first week I implemented the new plan, I had a breakthrough – not just in my grief, but in my state of mind and also my confidence. It was a life-changing period, even invigorating. It was like perceiving a soft fragrance of hope after living in darkness for a long time.

Instead of winging it day-to-day, trying to get the children to school and activities, then dragging them to events, I hired a college student to help at home. Stacy was a graduate student working on her master's degree in child life with a specialty in bereavement. She came two afternoons a week to play with the children. Sometimes she would help with bath time and homework. Most of all she gave me a much needed break to run errands alone or to accompany us around town providing an extra hand. Bringing in Stacy on a regular basis rather than relying on my friends and my Mom worked to restore my energy. No longer did I have to worry that I was burdening someone else with my responsibilities. No longer did I have to wonder whether help would be available when I needed it. I was able to sleep for three to four hours at night. And my appetite was growing.

I found a counselor who was able to give me tips on how to handle Anna Clare's anger. It was an almost indescribable relief to learn that everything I was experiencing with her was normal and could be fixed. Anna Clare's expression of anger and hate towards me was her manner of coping with the shock of having her Dad die. Anna Clare was intentionally refusing to allow herself to get emotionally close to me so that it wouldn't hurt as much if I died, too. The counselor told me every time Anna Clare screamed that she hated me, I was to continue reassuring her that I loved her anyway. As for the other girls, the counselor told me that if given proper care and discipline, all three girls would be fine. What a burden this took off my shoulders. I was on the right track with what I was doing and within a few weeks of following the counselor's instructions, Anna Clare's anger episodes transformed into her running to me in tears asking me to hold her.

I decided to add back into our schedule more of the children's regular activities. Ballet and swimming lessons were their favorites. Anna Clare liked play group with other moms and children. We spent more time having picnics at the park after school. I began to volunteer again in their classrooms.

There were other things I needed to do as well. There was a huge accumulation of mail to sort through and hundreds of thank you cards to be sent for the gifts I had received. Even though it would take innumerable hours, I set a goal. I wanted to have them complete by year-end so I could enter 2002 with a clean slate. I was going to need help. And as much as I liked to rely on myself, the past two and a half months had taught me there was a balance to be found between self-reliance and really asking for and accepting help when needed. I had learned God did not create us to live in isolation. The lives in each part of the community affected the others. It was okay – even proper – for everyone to have times when they were the recipient of help instead of the giver. So, I put pride aside and asked friends, church members, and the people at Thoratec to help me with this task.

There were additional mountains of paperwork, which only I could do. Over and above the regular household management paperwork (bills, bank statements, and the like), there was an overwhelming amount of material related to Tom's death to go through. Insurance policies, Social Security, government forms plus items as diverse as proposals from organizations looking to name awards after him to inquiries from around the world looking for more information about him and me. I was buried in it and had been for weeks. The difference was that now I was convinced the mess could be conquered, if I would just persevere and not give up. I had the time because I still wasn't sleeping all night. Finally I had a productive use for these otherwise seemingly endless wakeful hours.

Every night after the girls were tucked in bed I burned the midnight oil and slogged my way through another part of the pile, one paper at a time. Day-by-day, week-by-week I grew stronger in my confidence, in my convictions. I was making progress and it was empowering.

Next on my mind was my house, which was an unorganized wreck. Here I decided to concentrate on doing one thing at a time. I made a list and prioritized. Laundry one day. Pick up around the house the next. Another day to sort through the mail and pay bills. Only make phone calls which were necessary. Most phone messages went unreturned because whether with friends, family or well-wishers, phone calls seemed to average 45 minutes in duration and given the new commitment to my priorities, I couldn't afford the time. I tried e-mail, but found I received an average of 200 per day, making it impossible to respond to all of them as well. It wasn't easy. It was still hard to concentrate on tasks, and my organizational skills had been lost with the grief. I took it slowly.

The changes I made did not have to be large to be powerful. I learned that moving with a wise moderation which kept balance instead of extremes helped me get back on my feet faster. Instead of refusing the daily meals being brought by our church, I had them cut back to four meals a week. This enabled me to begin cooking for the family again but not all at once.

I decided to spend Christmas 2001 with my family in Arkansas. I let it be known I didn't want any gifts – that the focus was to be on the girls. The girls had received so many gifts from people that I began storing them instead of letting the girls open them. I would let them open the gifts for Christmas. Most of the gifts were still wrapped so I boxed them up and shipped them to Arkansas. There was no need to buy the children anything else. For the few gifts I did need to buy, I shopped online and in catalogues. Looking for special things actually helped take my mind off the daily grind.

I finally had set some initial goals and it felt good. The goals were simple: get through the holidays, be finished with everything I needed to do, and start the New Year with a brand new attitude and a more scheduled routine. For the first time, I looked at my life and my household and thought, "I am doing this!"

But progress is rarely a straight line from one point to another. In the real world there are generally sidesteps and even some backwards steps along the way. As could be expected, our lives continued to be punctuated periodically with reminders of the rough road we had traveled since September.

Before leaving for Arkansas, I went to Halley and Madison's kindergarten Christmas program in mid-December. There were dads with video cameras and moms taking pictures. All the kids were dressed in their holiday best. They sang Christmas carols and recited poetry. You could feel beautiful reverence for Christmas and holiday excitement. Tom's absence for me was pronounced.

When the program was over, all the children descended to find their parents in the seating area below. I made my way toward the stage, but noticed that Halley and Madison were exiting in opposite directions. I couldn't go in both directions at once, so I attempted to reach Madison. But the crowd was so thick I lost track of her, which meant she lost track of me. Suddenly I was surrounded by what it seemed like 10 different, well-meaning people, all telling me in a panic that Madison was trying to find me. "She's crying and very upset," someone said. "Can you stay here and let her find you?" said another.

"Sure," I said slowly, trying to remain calm. "But where's Halley?"

The girls had been running around the room, trying to find me. At first, from separate directions they had each made their way to where I had been sitting during the performance. When I wasn't there, they were terrified.

It took a few more drawn-out minutes to find each other. When we were finally all together, the girls cried and sobbed and hugged me tight. "We thought something bad happened to you, Mommy…. We thought something bad happened to you."

It was the first time I had seen them visibly panic in a crowd, even though we were in familiar surroundings. The fear of not knowing where I was and whether I was safe even for just a moment was unbearable for them. I struggled to keep my composure. I felt so bad for them. I held them both close as securely as I could and sent a prayer heavenward, "Please, please, please God, let me live long enough to see my children grown." I couldn't bear the thought of what losing their second parent could do to them.

The week before Christmas, we flew to Little Rock. My dad and step-mom picked us up at the airport, and we went to their apartment. My step-mom had a job in the city, so Monday through Friday, they stayed in town. My dad was retired, but on weekends, they still stayed at the farmhouse in Halley, Arkansas, where I had grown up. After we settled in, I started checking messages. Not surprisingly, even though I had clearly left a message on my answering machine that said I would be out of town until early January, there were numerous calls from reporters. Their messages all followed a typical pattern: "I know you're on vacation, but…if you have time, could you call me?" It was mostly print reporters and a few TV stations, but only one message prompted me to return the call.

The message was from ABC News. The network had created a new award, Hero of the Year. It was to be awarded to Tom, Todd Beamer, Jeremy Glick, C.C. Lyles, and Mark Bingham. They wanted me to appear on *Good Morning America* to accept the award in Tom's honor.

Flying to New York City was out of the question, but I was willing to do the interview live via satellite from the ABC station in town. Since it was live television, it should not require a big time commitment and all I had to do was say thank you. The shoot would take place early in the morning when the children would still be sleeping. The arrangements were made.

On December 21, a car picked me up and took me to the station. It was close, only 10 minutes away, and I was there by 6:00 a.m. While waiting in the green room, people passed by, whispering, "Who is she?" or "Why is she here?" Finally a woman asked me, "Do you know why they're doing a satellite with *Good Morning America*"?

"Yes, I'm going to be on."

"Oh, I'm so sorry." Then she walked off like she said something wrong. I quietly laughed.

Then another guy walked up to me and said, "Well, just who are you?"

I didn't feel like explaining myself and wanted to say, "I'm not anyone special." Instead, I gave enough information to explain my presence in the studio, "Well, my husband was killed on Flight 93 on September 11."

"Oh, oh, I'm so sorry. I didn't mean to offend you with my question."

I wasn't offended. "Not at all," I responded, "It's fine that you asked."

It was time to do the show. All of the nominees for the Hero of the Year award, which now included Mayor Giuliani, the heroes of Flight 93, and a few other names, received crystal trophies. I was asked a few questions. The one I liked best was "What do you think a hero is?"

My response was that being a hero is someone who, when faced with danger or a life-threatening situation, is able to act with courage and bravery to alter the situation. Tom believed very few people deserved to be called a hero. The fact that people were referring to him as one would make him feel honored. I was proud and honored to receive the award on behalf of my husband.

Quickly the interview was over and I was on my way back to the apartment. I was pleased. I was doing the right thing by making my priority be spending time with my girls.

Now though the holidays were on my mind. There were so many friends and family I wanted to see. I hoped I would have enough energy to visit with all of them. I also hoped I had reached the point where I could get through this first Christmas without Tom with some degree of decorum.

The next day, we drove to my dad's house in Halley. With only a few days before Christmas, I spent my time wrapping gifts, helping in the kitchen, and playing with the girls.

It surprised me that hardly anyone was stopping by the house to visit. When I asked my Dad, he told me that my family had told everyone I wanted to be left alone. While this wasn't entirely true, I had to admit the peace and quiet was a welcome change. However, I was glad to see so many people from the community at church the next day. Many of them were elderly people whom I addressed as my aunts and uncles. Though we were not actually related, I grew up with them being as close as family. Each one had either written letters or called since Tom died. This was my first opportunity to express my gratitude in person. I wanted to let them know how much their kind words and outpouring of love had meant to me these past months. I visited with as many of them as I could.

Christmas Eve day, carolers sang at our doorstep throughout the afternoon. It lifted our spirits and created a peaceful atmosphere in which to reminisce with friends and relatives about growing up in this small community. It felt so good to be home. It helped take my mind off Tom not being there.

Christmas Eve dinner was quiet and we turned in early. I was hopeful as I went to bed that Christmas wasn't going to be so bad after all.

Christmas morning the children woke up bright and early and raced directly into the living room. I was right behind them with my camera. The tree sparkled with colorful ornaments and glittering lights. Wrapped packages spilled out from underneath it in all directions. Suddenly, instead of reveling in the beauty of the moment, a chill came over me. *Tom's not here to see this.* The children began to tear open the gifts.

I found a reclining chair across the room and sat down. *Don't cry, Deena. The children are here. It's Christmas morning. They're happy right now. Be strong. It's important to be happy for the children.*

My grandmother, step-mom, dad, and sister came in and found a seat. Together we sat quietly watching the girls in their excitement. Anna Clare brought one of her toys over for me to see and nonchalantly commented, "Mom, I wish Dad was here to see my new toy." As she held it up, I forced a smile. Then she turned and ran back to the tree to open another gift.

Madison was next. She came over to me and asked, "Mom, are you missing Dad today?"

"Yes, honey, I am."

"Yeah, I am too, Mom." She sat on my lap for a few minutes while we watched Halley and Anna Clare open more presents. Then she went back to finish opening her own gifts.

The gifts for the adults still needed to be opened. My step-sister Kristen started passing them out. I looked down to see a stack growing at my feet.

Why would my family buy me so many gifts? Once the grandkids were born, we all agreed not to buy gifts for the adults. Only spouses exchanged gifts. Maybe they were trying to compensate for Tom not being here.

I thought about opening them, but decided I would wait. As the floor became littered with paper, I helped the children sort through which were whose. Finally at the encouragement of my family, I opened my gifts. Many were novelty items decorated with the American flag. While I appreciated the gifts and would put them to good use, they were yet another reminder that my husband wasn't there. He had died defending what the flag represented.

When all the gifts were opened, I chatted with the children about what they had received. Which gifts had they liked the best? Which ones were they going to play with first? To my surprise, the girls weren't interested in playing with any of their new toys. I asked Halley why.

"I don't know, Mom. I'm just so sad Daddy's not here."

I hadn't expected to hear that. I hadn't expected the children to be that aware, that sad. I had expected the gifts to absorb their focus as gifts normally did on Christmas day. I rose and left the room to regain my composure.

When I returned minutes later, the children's mood had lightened and they wanted to go outside. I busied myself finding gloves, boots, hats, and coats to dress them. A big part of Christmas was now over. The gifts were opened. Underneath the Christmas tree was cleared. All I had to do now was make it through the rest of the day. I could do this.

Once the children were outside, I went into my bedroom and whispered a quick prayer of thanks. I thanked God that we were together. I thanked Him that we had made it to my Dad's safely. I thanked Him that we were healthy and had food on the table. When I finished, I realized I had been so busy thanking Him, I had forgotten to ask for the one thing I thought I needed: His strength. Yet the more I prayed, the less I believed I needed to ask for strength. I was learning that when you seek to be continually in God's presence, you don't always have to ask for what you need because He has given it to you already.

I felt better. I felt stronger. I felt more peaceful. I made my way to the kitchen to see if I could help with the meal.

Cindy, my step-mom, lit a candle and said a prayer for Tom's soul prior to our sitting down at the table. It touched my heart. She asked for peace, comfort, and strength for us to face what we had yet to face. She also offered thanks for that which we had received that day. As it had been on Christmas Eve, the dinner was not uncomfortable, but quiet. Any conversation was mostly small talk.

After we finished, friends began to drop by to visit. They brought with them more gifts and desserts. Some came inside for coffee.

I excused myself briefly to call Mr. Tom and Mrs. Bev and wish them a Merry Christmas. They had opted to spend Christmas in Texas this year rather at home in Minnesota. I let them know I was thinking of them.

To me their voices sounded empty and alone. I wanted to wrap my arms around them and comfort them. Just as I was doing, their grief was something they had to work through on their own. And at some point each of us had to choose whether or not we would accept the peace and comfort from God for which others had prayed.

I took a deep breath and honestly felt like I was on my way back to being okay. I believed firmly that in His own sovereign, incomprehensible way, God had prepared me for what had happened to Tom. Even though I had experienced great physical shock and deep sadness – even horror at times – somehow, somewhere deep inside God now was giving me a sense of peace and renewed purpose. And I knew without a shadow of a doubt that God was going to take care of us.

Lying in bed that night I reflected on the day. I was on the road to recovery. We had made it through our first Christmas. I was so grateful. I remembered June whose husband had died in January. She had to wait almost a full year to go through her first holiday alone. Continuing my quest to find something good, I was glad Christmas had come early for us so we could move beyond it sooner. I also was glad to be with my family. It had been the best possible place for me to experience this day without my husband.

I realized with relief that the worst was behind me. I had made it through the media blitz, the memorials, the traveling, and the holidays. Now I could relax for a while and just enjoy my visit with family and friends. I could cry if I wanted to, be sad if I wanted to, and not have to live up to anyone else's expectations or be obligated to do things I didn't want to do.

Christmas night I slept well.

On December 26th I awoke before the children. I heard Dad cooking breakfast and went to be with him. On the way to the kitchen, I passed by the living room where the Christmas tree caught my eye, somehow barren without the presents beneath it. I stood there for a moment, suddenly aware of all the other holiday decorations as well. For some reason all of these now were a source of irritation to me, though I didn't understand why. When I saw my step-mom, as if echoing my thoughts, she suggested, "You know what, let's just put everything away today."

"Yes. That sounds like a good idea." And that's just what we did. My dad took down the outdoor decorations. Cindy, Kristen, and I put the tree away. I gathered all of the children's Christmas presents, boxed them up, and put them in the attic. They could play with them later. By noon, no more remnants of the holiday remained in the house. We were done with Christmas. We had made it through. Now it was time to move on.

Chapter Twelve

Making a Difference

"I am only one, but still I am one. I cannot do everything, but still I can do something. And because I cannot do everything, I will not refuse to do the something that I can do." – Helen Keller

Fighting For and Winning: The Cockpit Recording

The first time I requested the release of cockpit voice recording of Flight 93 was the afternoon of September 11th. Even then I felt that the families deserved to know what really went on up there, and I wanted to hear the tape for myself. When I visited the White House in October, I had mentioned my desire to hear the recordings to President George W. Bush as well. Later that month, Congresswoman Ellen Tauscher had visited me and asked if there was anything she could do. I told her I wanted to have the cockpit voice recordings released to the families. She said she would help. And she did.

Together, we each wrote several letters, made phone calls, and sent faxes to FBI Director Robert Mueller, requesting the release of the cockpit voice recorder. It was a slow process. We were fully into the New Year, and I still had no acceptable reply from the FBI. In fact, the only reply we had received was that releasing the recording could be detrimental to our mental health. I believed their concern to be insulting.

Representative Tauscher and I talked about the next step. "Should I go to Washington myself?" I asked.

"No. Let's send one more letter and see how they respond. It's only been six months. Perhaps they have reconsidered."

Only six months…. It seemed like an eternity for me, but I tried to be patient.

On March 20th, the day before my dad's birthday, Tauscher's office drafted another letter on my behalf. Again, we faxed it to the Director. In it, I made an even bolder move. I requested a personal meeting with the Director during the month of April. Perhaps he would have more difficulty turning me down in person.

We also sent the original copy of the letter via an overnight service for guaranteed early morning delivery.

The morning of the 21st, when I woke up, it was 10:00 a.m. in Washington, D.C. The Director should have received both the fax letter and the overnight package by now. I kept checking my messages to see if Tauscher's office had called with any news.

At 3:00 p.m. PDT I found a voice mail from Kathryn Turman with the FBI. "We received your letter, and the timing is good. Director Mueller has decided to let you hear the cockpit voice recording. Please call me."

I called her immediately, but couldn't get through. It was 6:00 p.m. on the East Coast. The offices were closed. But I was not to be deterred. I kept trying and trying and I managed to reach her three hours later – 9:00 p.m.–on her cell phone.

Kathryn said that Mueller had reconsidered, and that my letter had "good timing, very good timing." She also said I had an unknown advocate at the U.S. Attorney's office who felt strongly that we – the families of Flight 93 – deserved to hear the cockpit voice recording. She thanked me for my persistence, and because I had been so diligent, they wanted me to be the first to know.

A tentative date and place was set. April 18th in Princeton, New Jersey.

I asked her if we were going to hear an edited version or the recording in its entirety. "There will be no editing," she said, but then explained they had done some things to the tape to enhance some of the voices so we could hear them better.

I was excited. I thought about what I might hear. I was expecting to finally hear Tom's voice. All I could think about was I hadn't heard his voice in seven months. Now I knew I was going to hear it on April 18. I just knew I was going to hear his voice.

I spent Easter with my family in Arkansas. By the time we were back in California, the Burnetts and I had to talk seriously about the trip to New Jersey. Mr. Tom was coming with me. He had wanted to hear the recording all along, but I had doubts about whether Mrs. Bev would go. She said she wanted to try. She wanted to listen, no matter how hard it was going to be.

Her determination was both surprising and worrisome. Did she feel obligated? We didn't really know what awaited us emotionally on that recording.

The FBI had given us three and a half weeks to decide who would attend. We finally agreed to all go: Tom's parents, sisters Martha, Mary Margaret, and me. The trip also would include a visit to Ground Zero and the crash site in Pennsylvania. We would end the trip by claiming Tom's remains and escorting them back to Minnesota for burial.

I was getting nervous. The thought of leaving the children for five days didn't exactly thrill me either. I had not been away from them for more than a few hours since last September.

I decided to see how the girls would react to my being gone for a short period of time. There was an annual dinner at Pepperdine University in Los Angeles, to recognize those who made large donations to the school. They would also announce a scholarship in Tom's name and begin taking donations for an endowment. I would be gone for 17 hours.

Making this trip by myself would be good practice for the children and for me to prove to all of us that I could leave and come back. The girls were immediately afraid when I told them about the trip. They did not want me to fly on a plane. I tried to calm their fears, telling them it would only be for a few hours – less than a day – and that they could call my cell phone whenever they wanted. We also said the Safety Prayer.

On Tuesday, I flew down to attend the dinner with plans to fly home the following morning. The 45-minute flight was the longest of any I have ever spent in the air. Considering I was a flight attendant, who flew for a living, that says something about the tension I felt. When we landed in Los Angeles, my hands were sore from having gripped the arm rests so tightly. It wasn't that I was afraid the plane would crash and I would die. It was the fear of how my death would affect Halley, Madison, and Anna Clare. If 45 minutes in the air was this difficult, I wondered how I would endure a five-hour flight to New Jersey a week later.

The plan was for me to fly cross-country by myself to Princeton to meet the Burnetts. As I tried to get more comfortable with the idea, reporters were calling me to see if they could accompany me on the trip. Initially, I refused. But the more I thought about it, the more I realized that perhaps their company would prove a welcome distraction.

When I arrived at the San Francisco airport on Wednesday, April 17, I was greeted by the group of 15 people waiting for me. News reporters, photographers, and cameramen alike stated I had invited them to come along.

I didn't remember to whom I had talked, nor did I write down who was supposed to join me. Each asserted that it should be their exclusive and not the other's. Eventually we worked it out so everyone could come.

By the time we were three hours into the trip, I fully regretted my decision. I was distracted all right. They wouldn't leave me alone.

When I got up to use the restroom, each photographer stood up and either photographed or videotaped me walking down the aisle. When I returned to my seat, it was the same. They took pictures of me while standing, walking, and sitting.

The woman sitting next to me was staring. Finally she asked, "Are you a celebrity?"

I closed my eyes. Shaking my head, I said, "No, I am nobody. I am absolutely no one. I don't even know why they're taking those pictures of me."

She kept to herself while I looked out the window.

Mid-way through the flight, a CNN reporter approached. He asked to sit next to me and swapped his first-class seat with my seatmate. He wanted to know what my thoughts were about being on an airplane. Was this my first flight since September 11?

Before I had a chance to answer, a flight attendant brought me a note. It was from the captain, saying he saw my name on the manifest and that the crew was honored to have me on board. The note read that my husband was a great American hero, and that if there was anything he could do to make my flight more comfortable, to let the flight attendants know.

I appreciated his kind words, and shared the note with the reporter. He was surprised, so we talked about how things like that happen to me frequently. I elaborated how I receive random acts of kindness quite often. We talked about how people were effected on September 11 and how they have changed since. After a half-hour interview, I was exhausted. I excused myself and put on headphones to watch the movie.

We landed in Philadelphia, and I swapped one media swarm for another. This next group was from San Francisco Bay Area newspapers – the San Ramon Valley Times and the San Jose Mercury News.

I was accompanied by two photo-journalists while the rest followed in separate cars. The photo-journalists interviewed me for most of the two-hour drive to Princeton, talking at length about Flight 93, Tom's cell phone calls, and my quest to have the cockpit voice recordings released. By this time, I had been traveling for eight hours and had talked to at least 20 different reporters.

We arrived at Princeton around 7:30 p.m., and I checked into my hotel. The TV networks had been calling. Most of them were confirming tomorrow morning's schedule, but a few wanted to try to do an interview that night.

CNN's Greta Van Sustern was pressing hard for a three-way opposing opinion interview at 10:00 p.m. I was physically exhausted and emotionally wrung out, but I was more concerned with her interview style. In past programs I had noticed she often didn't let her guests fully answer her questions. I didn't want to put myself in a situation where I couldn't say what I needed to say. I had also learned about an article that day in the *Washington Post* saying that the pilots' union was opposed to the release of the cockpit voice recordings to the family members. I did not want to be asked about that story. And I certainly didn't want to be positioned in a debate with a third person. My answer to the interview request was no.

Her producers regrouped and called back. Would I consider a one-on-one interview? This was a better arrangement. I agreed. The interview lasted four minutes, and it went smoothly.

I returned to the hotel afterwards and tried to sleep. It was futile. All night my mind ran in circles thinking about what was going to happen the next day. I had been waiting almost seven months for this. Even though I was sure I would hear Tom's voice, I had a lot of time since March 21st to try to lower my expectations.

Keith had helped me. "Deena, I know you want to hear Tom's voice. I know you're looking for answers. But I want you to really think about the fact that you might not get either. This has been quite a project for you, and you need to go in there not expecting anything. That way when you walk out of there, anything you do find will be a gift."

All right. No expectations. Receive anything there as a gift.

His advice helped me convince myself I wouldn't recognize anyone's voice. I decided it would still be worth it if none of my questions were answered. I was thrilled about finally being able to hear, and relieved to know the FBI wasn't trying to hide anything from us. That felt like a real victory. I had done something. I had stood up for truth and the right thing was coming to pass.

The next morning I was out of bed early – 4:30 a.m. Alice Hoglan, the mother of Mark Bingham, and I had interviews scheduled on *Good*

Morning America and *The Today Show*. We had decided weeks ago to team up for the day.

The two of us went from one place to the other doing back-to-back interviews all morning. My cell phone rang incessantly as the hotel tried to reach me with additional interview requests.

At midday I made time to eat lunch at the hotel restaurant, but wasn't very hungry. Chips and dip were all I could manage.

A woman stopped by my table and introduced herself as Meredith Rothenberg, the wife of Flight 93 passenger, Mickey Rothenberg. I asked her to join me. My thoughts immediately went to her husband, who was seated in first class near Tom and the four hijackers. Based on my conversations with Tom, I had always thought it probably had been her husband who the hijackers knifed to death early on that day.

"I've wanted to talk to you," she said. "I know your husband told you that a passenger was stabbed by the hijackers. I think it may have been my husband."

I was stunned that we shared the same notion. "Why do you think that?" I asked.

"Mickey was the kind of guy who would have interfered," she said. "He was loud and friendly, and enjoyed talking to people who were visiting America. He would have welcomed them in a neighborly way and probably questioned them about why they were here. Had he seen something wrong going on, he would have stepped in and tried to negotiate with the hijackers – tried to get them to calm down and change their mind. He was a negotiator. It's what he did for a living. He would have tried to find out what they wanted and worked to achieve an end without violence."

Meredith added that her husband, like Tom, traveled all the time. "We talked on the cell phone several times a day, so he would have called me from the plane had he been alive," she said.

It all made sense. Her theory was right on target with mine. I remembered my conversation with Tom, who told me a passenger had been knifed. I knew the passenger who was killed had tried to interfere. I just didn't remember why I knew that. Tom must have said something. I couldn't remember his exact words and I had not written down the entire conversation the first time he called. More pieces of the puzzle were coming together. My instincts about what had happened on the plane that morning, the possibilities of which had played over and over in my mind through the months, were being confirmed. It was time to listen to the cockpit recordings.

Our session was scheduled from 1:30 p.m. to 5:30 p.m. There were nearly 125 of us seated in the room. It began with a series of preliminary speeches about what we could expect and what we were going to hear. They also told us that the information from the Flight 93 recording would be used to try and convict Zacarias Moussaoui, who at the time, was supposedly the fifth hijacker.

After the preliminary speeches were over, they separated us into family groups to conduct individual and family interviews to be sure that we wanted to hear the recording. They also needed to secure testimony from about 30 people, who would later serve as victim-impact witnesses at the Moussaoui trial.

Dave Novak, one of the U.S. attorneys prosecuting the case, asked me about the cell phone conversations. I happened to carry a transcript with me everywhere I went, so I handed him a copy. He was very interested in the transcript and asked if I had a recording of the conversations. I didn't.

He said he would most likely use the transcripts as evidence in the trial, and asked me if I wanted to be a guilt witness instead of a victim-impact witness. "I'll do anything I can," I said.

Tom's parents and sisters did most of the talking during the family interview. Mr. Novak was asking about what kind of person Tom was. He asked about his job and his travels. I couldn't speak. My emotions were all over the place. My head was spinning. The ground was moving. I was glad his family was there to handle the questions.

The family interviews ended at 4:00 p.m. We were running behind schedule. The listening session was next.

We were led back into the main room where Mr. Novak addressed everyone. "There will be a transcript of the recording projected on a large screen to make it easier to understand what you will be hearing," he said. He also told us there would be a timeline projected on the screen, so we could match the sounds to get a better idea of the scenario on the plane.

"We have translated all Arabic into English. You'll be able to tell whether it's an American voice or an Arabic voice by looking at the transcript."

He added that they did, in fact, know the exact target of the airplane, but as much as they wanted to share that information with us, they had decided against it. They wanted to see how well we could be trusted with the information we received today. "All I can say is that many lives were saved," he said.

At the time, the media suspected that the main target was the U.S. Capitol. (Months later, we learned it was the White House.)

They gave us headsets and dimmed the lights. Immediately several people around the room began to fuss, complaining they could hear nothing but static. The staff in the room worked quickly to trade out the headsets. The room became quiet.

We could feel the tension building. Every passenger was represented by at least one person and some by as many as five. The crewmembers' families had listened to the recording earlier that day.

The room was now dark, and the transcript was projected on the screen. There was no sound in my headset. They announced we could take notes, and I scrambled to get a notebook and pen from my purse, as did several other people in the room.

The recording started playing. The first voice I heard was a woman's. "I don't want to die, please, please, please don't kill me."

Reading the transcript it seemed she was pleading for her life, but listening to her voice, she seemed calm and speaking softly, trying not to upset anyone. I imagined her being held in an uncomfortable position with her head pulled back and a knife to her throat.

Then there was moaning. I could hear a woman moaning. But it wasn't an "I'm dying" kind of moan. It was an "I'm very uncomfortable" kind of moan. I never got the impression she was killed. It sounded as if she was gagged or bound in some way.

I also could hear the hijackers. They seemed frustrated, yelling at one another and at the passengers, telling them to "sit down, sit down, sit down, sit down." Shouting. Screaming.

It presented an image as if the hijacker was holding a knife to the woman, threatening to kill her and other people – passengers or crewmembers – were standing or slowly approaching him. The hijacker was yelling at them to sit down.

It wasn't clear where the pilots were. I never heard an American voice – other than the woman's – on that part of the tape.

The next thing I heard was that they had control of the cockpit. There were two hijacker pilots, and I could hear one instructing the other on how to fly the plane. It was obvious which one was in charge.

Alarms were going off in the cockpit. One hijacker pilot was yelling at the second, telling him he was touching the wrong buttons.

"Get the pilot back up here to turn off these alarms," he said. This let us know that one of the pilots was still alive.

The cockpit door opened and closed a few more times. But the alarm stopped before it was clear whether or not an airline pilot had been brought up from the back.

Next I heard the hijacker pilot on the intercom. He said, "This is your captain. Remain seated. We have a bomb on board. We are going back to the airport to meet our demands."

After that, I heard voices from the hijackers fussing at each other. Then more noises as another hijacker went in and out of the cockpit. I could tell the passengers were becoming restless because one of the hijackers said something to the hijacker pilot, who replied, "Well, hold the axe up. Just scare them."

"Should I take it out?" (Meaning, should I take the axe out of the cockpit?)

"No. Hold it up so they can see it through the window."

It was explained to us that the hijackers evidently thought the peephole in the cockpit was a window. They didn't realize it was a one-way view.

Then I heard the cockpit door open and close a few more times. Finally the pilot hijacker said, "What's going on?"

"They're fighting."

"Well, let the guys in. Let the guys in now." The pilot wanted all the hijackers in the cockpit, but I could never tell how many hijackers were up there at any given time.

The next thing I heard was intense fighting going on right outside the cockpit door. Dishes were breaking. Then I heard a chilling scream come from one of the hijackers, as if he was being killed. It was clearly one of the hijackers. Then he screamed again.

Right after I heard the second scream, an American male yelled, "In the cockpit, the cockpit."

It was Tom. It was so clearly, so unmistakably his voice. As soon as I heard it, I sat straight up.

My first impression was that Tom had killed that hijacker. When I realized what he had done, I remembered him saying that he knew he was capable of killing a person if he or his family were ever threatened. While I felt proud that he took the initiative to try to stop the suicide mission, I was also saddened that he had to experience taking a human life.

Then I looked at his parents and his sisters. They had recognized his voice, too. We were all looking at each other stunned and wide-eyed.

Even in the moment of realizing what was going on in the plane as he spoke, Tom's voice sounded so beautiful to me. I hadn't heard his voice in seven months. I didn't know how to react. I wasn't thinking about the horror he must have been experiencing. I was flooded with memories of our life. My life with him.

Then I heard the passengers grab one of the meal carts. They were using it to slam into the cockpit door. Again and again, I heard the dishes inside the cart shifting back and forth, breaking. I could hear other passengers yelling, chanting, the same instructions Tom called out before, "In the cockpit. In the cockpit."

Then someone yelled, "In the cockpit or we'll die."

Then the cockpit door gave way, and a male passenger yelled, "Stop him." A different male passenger yelled, "Let's get them."

When the cockpit door crashed open, an intense struggle followed inside the cockpit. Men were physically straining, scuffling around, but they weren't saying anything.

I imagined the hijackers with their knives drawn as one of the passengers reached in, grabbed the first hijacker, and dragged him over to the main cabin door to be pummeled.

There was more fighting outside the cockpit. Then I heard people back inside the cockpit trying to get the other hijackers out of their seats.

I heard one of the hijackers say, "Should I finish it off?"

Another hijacker said, "No, not yet."

It seemed like there was only one hijacker left in the pilot's seat. He shouted, "God is great."

Then I heard one of the passengers say, "I'm injured." as if to say, "I'm injured, keep going—go on."

One of the last things I heard was a male voice, an American voice, yell, "Roll it!"

Another passenger screamed, "Turn up!"

Then the plane crashed.

After the first listening session was over, almost everybody left. The intensity must have been more than they could bear or they had heard what they needed and didn't want to subject themselves emotionally to listen to it again. Only a small group of about 15 of us stayed for the second session.

I wanted to hear the recording again because, after hearing Tom's voice, my sobbing had interfered with my ability to listen carefully to the rest of the tape. And I did have to listen carefully. Many of the voices coming through the headset were difficult to make out. I had to rely on the transcript on the wall to make sense of some of the words.

As people were leaving the room, I found Alice and asked her if she had heard Mark's voice. She said, "No, I didn't. Well…I thought I heard him say, 'Oh man' but I'm really not sure."

I shared with her that I heard Tom's voice. That he had said, "In the cockpit! In the cockpit!"

"Oh, that's so wonderful. He was leading the way!" said Alice.

I walked over to Liz Glick and asked her if she had heard Jeremy. She had been crying. "He didn't say anything, but I could hear him grunting."

She smiled and we giggled together.

"Grunting? Was he a grunter?"

"Yes, he was a grunter," she said smiling through the tears.

I was very happy for her. I knew what it meant to hear something familiar, something that only she would recognize. It must have seemed strange to others for us to be so happy.

I looked around and saw a relative of Donald Green, who was the passenger pilot on board. I was curious to know if he made it to the cockpit. I suspected that if the passengers were going to have him fly the plane, they would have saved him until the very end. I had always assumed that the actual pilots were killed, but nothing on the tape confirmed this.

I asked Donald Green's relative if he had recognized Donald's voice in the recording. He shook his head; he hadn't.

I looked for Lisa Beamer, but she had already left.

During the first listening session, when family members heard different voices, they looked at each other wondering if it was their loved ones. Some of them debated back and forth. It wasn't like that for the Burnetts and me. We all heard Tom and recognized him. It was clearly Tom's voice.

I listened to the whole recording again. Alice and her brother Vaughn joined me. After the second listening session was over, I sat and reviewed my notes. Using them I started to play back in my mind what might have happened during the last few minutes of Tom's life. I now had a much better idea. The plane had crashed within 10 minutes after our last phone conversation.

Keith once described Tom as the kind of guy you gave the football to with five seconds left to go in the game. "Just give me the ball," Tom would say. "I'll get it in the end zone."

The plan would have been simple. First, rush the hijacker in first class. He was probably the one with the bomb strapped to him. Second, get into the cockpit and take back control of the plane.

Tom also would have encouraged everyone – both men and women – to take an active role. He would have told them what they were about to do would be a united effort, to act with honor and valor in completing each task. He would have told them that regardless of what it was, from storming the cockpit to sitting in their seats praying, each one of them had to perform their task well.

And so, when Tom hung up the phone, I imagined that he gathered everyone around him and said, "OK. Does everyone know what their job is? OK. All right. Let's go."

Then they went up the aisle. Mark Bingham, a big man, 6'4" 250 pounds, would have likely been in front. Tom would have been right behind him. Alan Beaven would have been there too. They were the biggest guys on the plane. Lou Nacke had to have been close. I understand he had a lot of upper body strength.

With his long reach, Mark would have grabbed the hijacker's hand that held the knife and stabilized the other hand while Tom bashed the hijacker's head with a water fire extinguisher.

As soon as Tom realized the hijacker was dead, he would have turned and yelled, "In the cockpit! In the cockpit!"

Then, using a meal cart, two or three large men started ramming the cockpit door. Because the cockpit door is so narrow, barely the width of a man's shoulder, they wouldn't have been able to get much leverage having one person ram into it. They also wouldn't want to risk injuring their biggest guy. Using a meal cart made sense.

Then Tom and Mark may have rushed into the cockpit. Fighting off the hijacker with the axe, they would have grabbed him and pulled him into first class to be pummeled by the other passengers.

Tom must have stayed with this hijacker. He was probably the one who said, "I'm injured." When I saw the phrase on the transcript, I thought it was something he would say. He would never say, "I'm hurt" or "I'm bleeding." He would have said, "I'm wounded" or "I'm injured." Not many people spoke that way, but Tom did.

With two hijackers down, Jeremy Glick, Lou Nacke, Alan Beaven, and others would have charged-in and wrestled control of the plane. With the remaining hijackers held at bay, one of the United Airlines pilots would have rushed in to fly the plane.

But there were too many factors beyond their control. The 757 is a big airplane, and because of its size, it doesn't react as quickly as they needed it to.

Flight 93 was flying too fast and too low to the ground. It was traveling faster than the speed of sound – over 625 miles an hour. The autopilot was turned off.

The plane's cruising altitude is usually 35,000 feet, but it was now only about 8,000 to 9,000 feet off the ground. Anything below 10,000 feet and under 200 miles per hour is considered a landing approach.

When the United pilot grabbed hold of the yoke, he probably wasn't seated because the plane was turned over on its right side. The right wing dragged the ground, forcing the nose downward, and the plane was vaulted, tumbling into the air and trees. Due to the high speed they were traveling, everything just disintegrated.

There simply wasn't enough time. It all happened in a matter of seconds. Everyone died a hero.

I felt a hand on my shoulder. "It's time to go, Deena," said Alice. The room lights were turned up. I nodded. Now I knew. I was glad it was finally over.

As we were leaving, Alice and I were told not to say anything to anyone about what we heard. Originally they said we could talk about any voices we recognized. Now the U.S. Attorney's office had changed their minds. We were not to say we had recognized our loved ones. *How was saying I heard Tom's voice going to affect the case?* I left the room unsure about exactly what to do.

Outside, there were mobs of reporters from all over the country, shouting and hurling questions. "How did you feel when you heard Tom's voice?"

"How do you know I heard Tom's voice?" I replied.

"Your sisters-in-law told us," another one said.

"They did?"

"Yes."

"Where are my sisters-in-law?"

The reporter pointed toward the other end of the courtyard. I saw Tom's parents, Martha, and Mary walking toward me. Martha was smiling, pointing at herself, saying, "I did it. I did it."

I raised my hands, gesturing why?

Martha said with a grin, "I didn't hear anyone say not to tell. I'm sorry, but I had already left the room when they changed their minds."

I was suddenly concerned. "Tell me, what else have you said? I need to know so I can answer these questions."

Mary whispered in my ear, "We said we heard Tom's voice. But that's it. We didn't want to be too specific."

The cameras were clicking as we discussed how much to share with the media. Then I turned to the reporters and simply said, "You know what? It's a beautiful secret. That's all."

Beautiful because I heard my husband's voice; secret because I can't tell you.

(The photographs taken of Mary and I when we were speaking made the front page of most newspapers across America. We were portrayed as sharing a tender moment.)

I wanted to get out of there, and I wanted to be left alone. I dodged a few more questions and went to find our car and driver. The reporters were right on my heels.

The car wasn't where it was supposed to be. Someone said the police had made everyone move their cars.

Those of us who stayed for the second listening session came out later than scheduled. We were supposed to be done by 5:30 p.m., and it was now past 7:00 p.m.

I began to panic. The reporters were still after me. I had to do something to make the situation more manageable, so I decided to answer their questions.

On the way to the podium with all the microphones, a New York Times reporter trailed me wanting to know detailed information. I knew everything I said would end up in the paper the next day, so I tried to be vague. He was forceful, and continued to press me to tell him what I heard. Could I confirm this? Could I confirm that?

Someone must have already provided him with a lot of information. I was surprised at how much he already knew. Finally I said, "I just can't answer those kind of questions, period. Why don't you go talk to Alice?"

"I already have," he said. He walked away in a huff.

At the microphone, the reporters began lobbing questions at me. I was answering as fast as I could. When I started talking about the hijackers, Vaughn came over to me and whispered, "It's time to go." I realized I shouldn't say anything more.

I packed my bags and met Alice and Vaughn in the lobby. A car was waiting to take us to New York City. We had a number of interviews scheduled for the next day, starting very early in the morning.

We arrived at the new hotel after 11:00 p.m., and I couldn't sleep much that night. I was tossing and turning, replaying the sounds of the cockpit voice recording. I was exhausted. *Is it going to be like this every night?*

Visiting Ground Zero and the Shanksville Crash Site

I woke at 4:30 a.m. and tried to gather my strength for the day ahead. The interviews were the least of my worries. I knew what to say. Today was the day we were visiting Ground Zero and the crash site.

The plan was to do the morning interview shows, visit Ground Zero, and then catch a flight to the crash site in Pennsylvania.

Between 6:30 a.m. and 10:30 a.m. Alice and I pre-taped for NBC's *The Today Show,* did two live interviews for ABC's *Good Morning America* and *The Early Show* on CBS, an interview for CNN with Paula Zahn, pre-taped a show for Fox, and then rushed over to MSNBC studios for another live interview.

I met the Burnett family back at the hotel. From there, we all went by subway to Ground Zero. The visit would be our first.

We were received in the "family viewing room" on the 20th floor of a building that used to be the World Trade Center. A miniature model of the former seven buildings was on display in the corner of the room to help us put things into perspective.

The view was expansive, but it was hard to imagine it was big enough to be 16 acres. I started to focus in on the pit below, watching the movement of the construction workers and trucks. I quickly realized just how small they were relative to the surrounding buildings.

A wave of nausea hit me. I imagined all those people trapped underneath, like Laurie's husband. I was overwhelmed.

As I sought to take in the entire scene, an image of two huge steel beams in the shape of a cross caught my eye. I inhaled sharply. Whether erected by God as the rubble fell or by man afterwards, it was amazing to see this great symbol of God's omnipotent love and provision overshadowing this desolate place.

In the viewing room itself, photos and cards covered the walls. There were thousands of them plastered everywhere. Tears began to fill my eyes. It was impressed on me again how September 11th wasn't just about the 3,000 people who died. It was also about 3,000 families like ours who were experiencing the same loss we felt every day.

We were not the only ones suffering. It had been too easy to forget how many other people were involved when our loss had been so personal.

Mary seemed to sense what I was feeling, "We can think of 9/11 as a day that this many people were lost, or we can think of it as a day this many people were saved because of what happened on Flight 93." She spoke to what I was thinking. "You know, there could be a room like this in Washington, D.C. over looking the White House…"

I began to understand the broader scope of the significance of Tom's heroic choice on the plane that morning. Yes, there were many families coping without their loved ones, but there were also many moms and dads who still went home to their children every night because of what Tom and the other passengers and crew did on Flight 93.

We didn't stay much longer. Our flight to Pittsburgh was leaving soon, and dark clouds were rolling in.

As it turned out our flight to Pittsburgh was canceled. We didn't want to delay the trip, so we opted to have the driver transport us by car to Shanksville. Six car loads of press followed us.

It should have only taken four hours to get to Shanksville, PA, but it took seven. The driver got lost.

We arrived late and checked into a small, quirky hotel. It was rural and quiet. I began to weep.

The next morning after breakfast, we met the Burnetts' family friend, Monsignor Joe from Iowa. He had come specifically to accompany us to the crash site.

As we approached it, my heart began to race. The crash site was large (about a 40-acre plot), private, and guarded. Only family members were allowed to enter the site itself. On one end of the plot was a memorial overlooking where the plane crashed. I could still see the slit in the earth where the wing had dragged.

Our car drove on a gravel driveway all the way into the memorial. Flowers, flags, and notes lined the make-shift road.

When I got out of the car, all I could hear was the wind blowing across the grassy fields. I looked up and saw the clear blue sky. Clouds billowed in over the hills, and the trees gently swayed in rhythm with the wind.

I had a vision of a plane flying overhead. On that plane were my husband and many other people. They were experiencing a terrifying situation, and then that plane began to fall out of the sky. I closed my eyes.

None of us could pretend anymore that Tom was on a business trip. This was the place where he died. Tom was gone. Now it was real.

I found a strange peace knowing this was Tom's resting place. What a fitting way for Tom to die. He didn't die sitting behind a desk at a publicly traded corporation. He didn't die watching TV in his recliner at his suburban home. He died fighting as a citizen soldier. What a fitting place for him to come to rest – an open field within a forest, so very similar to the Gettysburg battlefields which so fascinated and inspired him.

Tom had thrived on the outdoors. He loved the tranquility and beautiful God-given order that nature offered. It was a place to breathe deep and inhale peace. It was a place to be alone with his thoughts. Tom had spent so much time at our farmhouse in Wisconsin precisely for the feeling I got standing in this place.

Tom had done his job. I would continue to move forward and do mine. I began to recite the Safety Prayer that the girls and I would say in the morning.

I prayed that God would walk with us and hold our hands throughout the entire day, especially when we were apart from each other. I prayed that in the evening, we would be joined together again and would be safe. I prayed that God would make sure I made it home safe to my children.

The site was also visible to several farms in the area. Some of the neighbors drove down when they saw us approaching. They knew we were family members from the black limousines United Airlines provides for visiting families.

The locals had been deeply affected by the crash. Before September 11, these people lived a peaceful life. Now they had notoriety. Many of them actually witnessed the crash, and they often felt the need to connect with family members to heal and understand what happened.

As I turned to go back to the car, a woman approached and hugged me. She was one of the locals who saw us drive up.

"I've been praying for you, Deena, and I want you to know that God is going to take care of you," she said.

How did she know who I was? How did she know what to say?

Four times, within a short period of time in October 2001, people, who did not know each other, had spontaneously delivered the same message to me. It had become a symbol of God's provision for me even though Tom was gone. I was momentarily overcome with emotion and had to turn away.

I regained my composure and thanked her. Then I excused myself and headed for the reporters. I was going to talk to them. No one was ever going to forget the sacrifice Tom and his fellow passengers made for us.

Unfinished Business and Moving On

After hearing the cockpit recordings, I felt like I had reached a kind of peace, more of a coming-to-terms with what had happened. Yet I was determined that the world should know more about the heroes of Flight 93. Using Tom's actions as motivation, I wanted to fight for something good to come out of the tragedy of 9/11. I was going to do things I never had imagined.

The Burnetts and I escorted Tom's remains to Minnesota then I caught a plane back to California. Four weeks later, I returned to Minneapolis for Tom's funeral. This was the third memorial service for Tom in eight months. I decided not to take the children.

Even though the girls seemed to be doing well now, taking them to their father's funeral eight months after he had died might be confusing to them. This was affirmed when the girls overheard me talking on the phone about funeral preparations. After I hung up, Madison approached me and asked, "Mama, if Dad is in Heaven, how can we bury him?"

I thought carefully about what I was going to say.

"When you go to Heaven, God only takes your soul – the things that make you smile, the things that make you laugh, that make you who you are. These are the parts that go to Heaven. It's your body that stays on earth, and your body is buried," I explained.

On May 26, 2002, Tom received a military funeral, given to him based on his actions on Flight 93. He was buried at Fort Snelling in Bloomington, Minnesota. The Burnetts and I had wrestled with the idea of accepting the gift of a military burial. I knew Tom would not have agreed with our decision. He believed military service was very different from civilian life. He would have been humbled to have put himself on the same level as a person serving his country professionally. He would have seen his actions as those of a good citizen, not a soldier. But it was our decision. It was a great honor. We believed he deserved it.

As the limousine approached the burial site, soldiers representing every branch of the U.S. military lined the cemetery roadway. Hundreds of people stood behind each row of soldiers. Cameras in the distance came closer as the car stopped. Tom's family and I walked over to the canopy that shaded the plot and stood beside our seats.

The sun was shining. The wind was still. I was taken by the silence of my surroundings. For the multitude of people in attendance, all I could hear were the birds chirping in nearby trees.

Monsignor Joe welcomed everyone and said a prayer, but I couldn't listen to his words. It was beyond my capacity to comprehend them right now. There was the casket before me. Part of my husband was in there. I found being in its vicinity unexpectedly difficult. It had been eight months since his death. I had made strides along my path of grief, yet today, the grief hit me as if it were new again. Tom had been my beloved, beloved husband. I turned my thoughts toward his remains. I wanted to know what was inside. I couldn't stop thinking about it. But the casket was sealed. We had never been told any specifics about which remains of Tom were found. All we knew was that whatever was inside had been identified as Tom's via fingerprinting. His wedding ring was never found so I could only assume they had retrieved at least part of a hand.

The air cracking from a five-gun salute, representing each branch of the military, startled me. They fired their guns three times. *Taps* wafted through the air as young marines folded the flag with pride and precision. They gave it to an old soldier who had probably fought in World War II to deliver to me. It was surreal to have this man who had served his country so well standing before me and thanking me for what Tom had done. The presentation of the American flag to me by someone who had given so much to their country made me feel incredibly humble.

I was so proud to accept such a beautiful symbol, knowing that the United States of America believed my husband to be worthy of draping his coffin with a flag that hundreds of thousands of people had fought for. I was so proud of what Tom had done. He had earned the military honor and I was glad other people felt the same way.

Roses were laid on Tom's casket before it was lowered into the ground. The music came to an end. Silence. The funeral was over. It seemed like it had only lasted a few minutes.

After the service, as we drove out of the parking lot, people got out of their cars and men saluted us as we passed by. The finality of it all began to weigh heavily.

From Minnesota, I flew to southern California to be a guest on Rev. Robert Schuller's weekly television program the "Hour of Power," one of the longest-running shows on television with a worldwide viewing audience of 32 million people.

The Crystal Cathedral, where the show was taped, is an immense structure rising out of the ground like a rough-cut diamond, festooned with 10,000 windows, large video screens, and a ten-foot-tall angel hovering from the roof on a rope of gold. Since it was Memorial Day weekend, this Sunday's program was going to commemorate veterans and hold a special tribute to those who died on 9/11. Dr. Schuller had read that Tom was a citizen soldier. He wanted me to talk about the role Tom's faith and mine had played on that dreadful day.

Unbeknownst to him, Dr. Schuller was one of my childhood mentors. He was the author of *Move Ahead With Possibility Thinking*, the book which had helped me so much when I was 14 and my parents had just divorced. Through years of practice, I had learned to live with the message of that book. Those teachings served me well in dealing with Tom's death.

I was thrilled to be sharing the stage with a man whom I admired so much. I briefly told Tom's story, emphasizing how he had told me to pray. I also talked about Tom's faith.

"Tom had a sweet, loving faith in God," I said. "He went to daily Mass and was very prayerful." There was no doubt in my mind that Tom prayed before going down the aisle and into the cockpit of that airplane on 9/11.

Dr. Schuller asked how my faith had changed since Tom's death.

"I have come to rely on it even more for strength and for guidance than before. I spend more time in prayer, and I have a tendency to listen more carefully in trying to understand what God is saying to me."

Dr. Schuller went on to ask if I had been angry that God did not save him.

"No," I could honestly answer, "Because I think what happened was part of a plan that was greater than Tom or myself."

Dr. Schuller smiled lovingly and said, "It's called perfect Christian love, Deena. The love God has for you. And the perfect love you shared with your husband."

He held out his hands, signaling that the interview was over. I took them, smiled gently, and walked off the stage.

There were other good things – right things – going on during spring and early summer 2002 as well. In October 2001 I had been contacted by baseball player, Jamie Moyer and his wife, Karen. They wanted to know if I was interested in working with them to establish bereavement camps for children who had had a parent die. The idea was inspired by all the children who lost a parent on 9/11 like my three. However, the camps would serve all children who had experienced the death of a parent. I liked the idea of these camps. I had been looking for something like this for Halley, Madison, and Anna Clare, but all of the existing camps were structured for the children to come without their surviving parent. I knew that my girls and I would want to go together, that the stress level would be much less and the ability to enjoy much more if I were nearby. The camps the Moyer Foundation were proposing would enable the children to come with or without their surviving parent, whatever worked best for the child.

Now in the spring, the first bereavement camp was set to open. The Moyers allowed me to decide on the name. They would be called "Starbright"...Tom had been my shining star so it seemed appropriate. Initially, the four camps were able to handle 12-15 children each session. The sessions were once a week for six weeks during the school year, and a week long during the summer. After each session, the camps were able to expand to accommodate more and more children. The camps were located in New Jersey, Connecticut, New York, and Minnesota. The locations were chosen so they would be accessible to the 9/11 families, but they were open to anyone needing the service. We set up the "Tom Burnett Memorial Campership Fund" to provide an endowment for each of the camps to allow children to attend free-of-charge. The camps were operated by local hospitals, hospices, and bereavement groups. Each of the staffs consisted of doctors and professional bereavement counselors. We had done the right thing. We had identified a need and had executed a plan to meet that need.

Back home in San Ramon, it was the girls' last week of school in more ways than one. It had been a difficult decision, but I had decided that we needed to be near family. Since I had grown up in southeast Arkansas and my family was still there, returning home made sense. I chose Little Rock as opposed to my hometown of Halley because the city offered more choices in schools and activities for the children. Besides, Tom had always told me that if anything ever happened to him, the girls and I should go home to my family. In this way, the matter had been settled long before he died.

The girls were excited because they thought of the move in terms of going on vacation. They couldn't grasp the permanence of my decision, but rather asked questions about timeframe. How long would we be gone? When would we see our friends again? Soon they realized that what we were doing was quite different from other vacations because there were going-away parties, tearful good-byes, gifts exchanged, and of course the packing.

My mom, who had moved from Florida to California to be near us just before Tom died, decided to move as well.

The day we arrived in Little Rock was hot and humid – at least 100 degrees. Since the movers were still en route, we stayed with my dad and step-mom. When I told them back in January that I had decided to move there over the summer, they sold their house in Halley, and permanently moved to Little Rock to assist me in raising the children. It seemed the entire family was circling the wagons in an effort to help me.

The children were whining, sweaty, and sticky, asking to take a bath every hour. They had never experienced this kind of weather. Every time I turned around it seemed they were playing outside in the water or sitting in the bathtub trying to cool off. And then there were the mosquitoes.

I was anxious to move into the new house. Tom and I had spent the better part of two years searching for our dream house in California. When I began house hunting in Arkansas at Christmas-time, I simply used the same criteria that he and I had established: five bedrooms, three baths, a 3-car garage, and a large private yard. Tom had also insisted on a gated community ever since the first house we purchased. With his traveling so much, Tom had thought the girls and I would feel safer. I kept this in mind during the home search in Arkansas now that he was gone.

On the third day, the movers called and said they would meet us at the new house at eight o'clock the following morning. As we pulled into the community, I could see them in my rearview mirror, strategically positioning their huge truck through the small gate. The girls and I went ahead, knowing the truck would eventually find its way.

All three girls jumped out of the car and bolted up the steps of our two-story, red brick house as soon as I parked. They threw open the tall white doors. I heard them running from room to room. "It's just like in the photos," Madison yelled. "Mama, where are you?"

The house was much larger than what we were accustomed to. I found Halley in the library off to the left of the downstairs foyer. "Oh Mom, Dad would love this," she said. "It would hold all of his books."

While we didn't have a lot of furniture, we had a lot of stuff. The movers were soon drenched in sweat from unloading the boxes. Our air conditioning wasn't working yet. We opened all the windows in the house to help cool it down with no tangible results.

My morning consisted of telling five men where to put our belongings, running back and forth to the store to get snacks for the kids, and arranging for phone service and cable.

My cell phone kept ringing. Friends from California were checking in on me. Locally, different family members and people with whom I'd grown up were calling to welcome me to Arkansas.

The door bell rang. A little girl stood before me with a tray of Jello. "It's for the children," she said. We didn't have a refrigerator yet, so I had nowhere to put the Jello. I called the girls inside, who were playing in the backyard, but the Jello had melted all over the white kitchen counter before they could dig in.

In a few hours, Dad came to get the girls. I knew they were tired and not having much fun without toys or playmates. It was great having Dad so near by. It affirmed one of my reasons for re-locating.

The rest of the day, it was just the movers and me. At sunset, I was alone. I sat down in the kitchen and felt overwhelmed. Boxes were everywhere. I had no idea where to look for linens to make the beds. The food was eaten. And the house was still hot from the doors being open all day. I decided to return to my Dad's to spend the night. The boxes could wait.

The next morning, I teamed with my sister, sister-in-law, and two childhood friends. Together we made our way back to the house to begin unpacking. I didn't know where to start.

The first box I opened in the library was filled with Tom's business books. I read each title. "Influencing Integrity," "Transforming Leadership," "Productive Workplaces," "Thinking Strategically." I remembered when he had read each one. My thoughts drifted back to his studies at Pepperdine where these books were recommended reading. I looked up and noticed my sister-in-law had unpacked three boxes while I was reminiscing over one. I was not being very productive. So I gave up and decided to start in the bedroom.

Before moving, I had packed all of Tom's things in plastic containers. This way they could go directly into the attic and not be unpacked in the new house. However, I opened up boxes that I thought were my things, and I discovered a few additional things of Tom's that I had missed: a Casio diving wristwatch, a pair of khaki dress socks, his blue robe, and a few music CDs. I lingered over them, my mind drifting.

Tom wore that wristwatch when we vacationed in Mexico before the kids were born. The khaki socks were last worn to church the weekend before he left. I always had worn the blue robe when he was out of town because it made me feel closer to him. And the music CDs he had just purchased. They still had the plastic wrap on them.

I was called downstairs by my team of helpers. In the kitchen there were boxes stacked everywhere. They wanted to know into which cupboard they should unload the canned goods. I sat down in a chair, staring at the cabinets, trying to decide where the dishes should go, the glasses should be placed, and what to do with the Tupperware. I must have taken too long to answer because they soon took matters into their own hands and began filling the shelves.

I was so exhausted and overwhelmed I was just happy they were making the decisions instead of me. They were enjoying themselves at my expense. They poked fun at how many dishes I had: three patterns with 16 place settings each. They laughed about the plastic cups from Applebee's, which most people threw away. While I sat in the chair and watched in a daze, the three of them unpacked the entire house. I was so thankful.

A week later, on the 8th of July, I attended ESPN's ESPY awards in Los Angeles. ESPN was giving the Arthur Ashe Award for Courage to four men from Flight 93. Tom was one of them and I agreed to receive it on his behalf.

The day leading up to the award ceremony I was treated like royalty. I was assigned a limousine and driver and taken to a celebrity stylist to have my hair cut and make-up done. I had a manicure and pedicure in my hotel room. An old flight attendant friend came over for lunch and stayed the afternoon. The day was topped off by dressing in a beautiful black evening gown and walking down the red carpet into the Kodak Theatre.

In the Green Room, the four of us accepting the awards waited for our speeches. We each were handed one sheet of paper with our speech on it. They had composed speeches for us to convey what the producers wanted. The speeches were short and thematically tied together. But when I looked over my script, I knew I couldn't say the words they had written for me. I asked the writer for a pen. Turning the paper over, I wrote down a few sentences and handed it back to him. "This is what I want to say."

The ESPN representatives in the room – the executive producer, two vice presidents, and several writers – exchanged quick glances at one another. Then the lead writer looked down, read what I wrote, turned to me, and said, "It's exactly what you should say."

Backstage staff scrambled to get it to the teleprompter. One of them yelled, "Make sure the cameraman man knows to get a close up of Tom's parents in the audience."

I noticed the other recipients looking at each other, wondering if they should change their lines.

Soon, there I was, seated in a room filled with celebrities. In front of me were Serena Williams and Barry Bonds. To my right were Mathew Perry and Brooke Shields. But I wasn't nervous. I didn't even know who most of the people around me were. The theater itself was so much smaller than it looked on television. The program began. When it was time to accept the Arthur Ashe Award, the four of us stood side-by-side on stage, taking turns speaking. I was third.

The four men you honor tonight, died as heroes to millions. What I want you to know is they were much more than heroes. My husband, Tom, was a man of faith, heart-felt compassion, integrity, and love. He had a keen sense of right and wrong and believed morals and values were not debatable. These were virtues taught and demonstrated by his parents...making his actions on Flight 93, a tribute to his mom and dad. You see courage is not just one virtue; it is a culmination of all your virtues. It is not likely any of us will ever find ourselves in the position in which Tom, Mark, Todd, and Jeremy found themselves on the morning of September 11th, and so we cannot emulate their last acts. But we can emulate how they lived with faith, honor, integrity, and love.

It had been the first day I didn't feel sad all day long. It had been a good day, a really good day.

It was now almost a year since Tom's death. We had a new home, a new community, and a new church. My family and I were close, but the girls and I hadn't made many new friends. Because of my travel schedule, we had only been to church twice. We had not met our neighbors. And we still needed furniture to fill the empty rooms. This led me to think of our farmhouse in Wisconsin. It was something that had been nagging at me for quite a while because there were things, valuable things, which I needed to retrieve: an antique twin bed for the girls, an old wooden kitchen table, dishes and cookbooks that belonged to my grandmother, and cross-stitched samplers given to me by friends. Tom had been the last person there. The farmhouse was still winterized. I didn't want these things to get damaged or stolen over the summer.

I called Tom's parents and said the girls and I would be driving to Minnesota to visit them. On the way there I realized that we were never going to use the farmhouse again. I need to bring closure to that place. It would be one more change in our new life.

When we walked inside, seeing everything, the memories flooded back. I decided to be brave and not allow the emotion of emptying the house to overcome the reason for being there.

Of everything in the farmhouse, one of the most special items was a cross-stitched sampler that hung on the wall over Tom's beside table. It read:

> *"This is the beginning of a new day. God has given me this day to use as I will. I can waste it or use it for good. What I do today is important, because I'm exchanging a day of my life for it. When tomorrow comes, this day will be gone forever, leaving in its place something that I have traded for it. I want it to be gain, not loss; good, not evil; success, not failure; in order that I shall not regret the price I paid for it."* – W. Heartsill Wilson

I wondered if Tom read it before he left that last weekend.

With trailer in tow, the return to Little Rock was a hard two-day drive. Back home I was glad to put the antique twin beds in Anna Clare's room and have a kitchen table to use. Other than a sofa, the kitchen table was the only furniture downstairs.

Halley had a mattress set on a frame. Madison was still without a bed.

The next day Madison came to me crying and said, "It's hot here. I'm covered with mosquito bites. I have no friends to play with. And what's worse, I don't even have a bed to sleep in."

I concealed a smile.

"One of those things I can fix," I said. She had always wanted a canopy bed, so I ordered one out of a JC Penny catalog along with a set of dresser drawers and linens. Everything was delivered three days later.

For the time being, the rest of the rooms remained empty. Decorating would come later. It didn't seem important at the time. Top of my mind was making the transition for the girls into Little Rock as smooth as possible. I wanted to meet people at the church; moms whose kids would be attending school with mine. At a church picnic, I met two women with children the ages of Halley and Madison. Another lady, named Judy, had twins the age of Anna Clare. Judy had written to me while I was living in California. Her husband had grown up in southeast Arkansas, too. Our mothers had even worked together in the same hospital. We introduced the kids and they played, happy to have met children their own age.

As it turned out, everyone in Little Rock knew Judy. She guided me through Little Rock's social channels and made it easy to fit in. She invited me to everything from ballets to charity events and encouraged me to volunteer in the political scene.

Little Rock had been our home for about five weeks now. With the one-year anniversary of 9/11 approaching, media inquiries picked up again. I tried to accommodate most of the reporters' requests for interviews and updates on our lives. They came from everywhere: the San Francisco Bay area, the major New York broadcast networks. Morning shows and nightly news program representatives and international news agencies from Spain, Japan, Germany, England, and New Zealand. Not allowing them to interfere with our family life, I scheduled them around the kids' activities. If I was taking the girls to the park, the reporters could come along and video us from the background. If we were cooking dinner, the same rule applied. Trying to accommodate them all and speak to their audiences respectively proved emotionally draining.

I hoped that once the first anniversary was past my life would regain some normalcy. My life had once been consumed by laundry, housework, and simple errands to run: groceries, dry cleaning, shopping at the mall. Now those things were done only when absolutely necessary and always as an afterthought when they could be squeezed in.

Instead, my life now was filled by having the weight of the world on my shoulders. I listened to the news, the coverage about the war on terror. I felt the burden for every soldier that was killed, knowing that September 11 was the reason for each of the deaths. I worried about being the sole provider for the children. I worried about the decisions I made that impacted all of our lives. I was afraid, really afraid, of not doing everything exactly right in raising my children. Prayer and trusting God to give me strength and wisdom was the only way I could relieve some of that burden.

One of the bigger concerns during the summer of 2002 was whether to file a lawsuit against United Airlines. There was a deadline from the time of the crash by which the suit had to be filed and if we were going to do it, time was running out. I knew most of the 3,000 families who had suffered a loss were accepting the government compensation fund designed to prevent 9/11 families from suing the airlines instead. This fund was established because Congress was afraid so many lawsuits would put two of the three major airlines out of business, devastating our country's transportation system. I did not want to be part of causing that devastation.

I wanted to know how the hijackers got into the cockpit. Because the cockpit voice recording is a never-ending loop only recording the last 30 minutes of the flight, the sounds did not reveal how the cockpit door was opened. The hijacking was already underway when the 30-minute audio began.

Since I knew the hijackers didn't break into the cockpit, how did they get in? Who opened the door? Where was the breakdown in security? In communication? I needed answers.

Thus my unanswered questions helped sway my decision. I didn't know of any other Flight 93 family members who were going to file against the airline. I felt it was up to me.

The court system would provide answers. On August 5, Tom's parents and I filed the lawsuit against United Airlines and Argenbrite, the security company responsible for screening at the Newark airport on September 11.

On the heels of the United lawsuit, just one week later, Tom's parents and I filed suit for $1 trillion against financial supporters of terrorist networks. One hundred fifty defendants were named, ranging from individuals to banks to charities, in seven different countries. There were even members of the Saudi Arabian Royal Family. This was another way for us to do the right thing and fight back.

In November 2001, I had contacted an attorney, Ron Motley, about recourse through the court system for the terrorist actions which had taken my husband's life. Tom's dad wanted to sue Al-Qaeda and Osama bin Laden. Mr. Tom believed putting a strong-hold on their finances would weaken the terrorists' ability to escape our government. Ron Motley said he would consider the case.

As it turned out, a World Trade Center widow, Joanne Havlish, filed that lawsuit in December 2001. When Ron called and shared this news, he suggested we join her lawsuit and said he would sign on as co-counsel. We agreed.

As part of their co-counsel, Ron and his team were privy to much legal and financial information about how the Al-Qaeda was funded. He told us we could file a separate lawsuit against people who provide money to the terrorists. By doing so, we could not only severely impact the finances of Al-Qaeda, but every terrorist organization in the world.

Our position was simple. Any person or organization who had *knowingly* given money to a terrorist organization for any reason would be named as a defendant. As the attorneys began researching possible defendants, the list grew longer. Although we didn't know whether our efforts would be successful, we had to try. We believed it was the right thing and one way we could fight back.

On August 11, Ron called and asked if the Burnetts and I could be in Washington, D.C. the next day to announce the suit. With only a few hours to pack and find a babysitter, I managed to catch the flight. The girls would stay with my family.

When we arrived at the JW Marriot, we thought it was going to be just the three of us meeting with Motley. But there were hundreds of people at the hotel who had signed on to this lawsuit via their own attorneys.

We were stunned. What we thought was going to be a simple press conference turned out to be a media frenzy. We stood on stage behind Motley as he announced the suit. Mr. Tom gave a short statement outlining the reasons for filing. Then it was my turn. I stated what we hoped to accomplish. Then one by one, attorneys, legal assistants, took the microphone and explained why they signed on as counsel.

As I stood listening to the questions from the news reporters and the answers from the attorneys, I looked at my watch. Several hours had passed. I had a plane to catch. So I walked off the stage and left. I wasn't going to spend another night in D.C. My children were waiting.

Sitting on the airplane, I wasn't sure what I had done. I didn't know anything about the legal system. I didn't know what kind of proof Ron Motley had against the defendants. But I knew I had to do something.

In the days that followed we were kept abreast of the suit through conference calls and emails. Because there were 7,000 plaintiffs, we decided to have a core group of people vote on decisions regarding the suit. I was named by the attorneys to both the executive committee and the steering committee.

With hundreds of thousands of documents, it was difficult to grasp all of the information. Because of the sources from which we were getting the information, some of it couldn't be shared via telephone. The attorneys had their phones tapped. They were careful not to use cellular phones and made it clear to us not to use ours when discussing the case. They were adamant that I understood my family and I could be in danger for pursuing this course of action. In the beginning they wanted us to be aware of our safety at all times.

Because they wouldn't share the information via fax or phone, I flew back and forth to Washington, D.C., often for briefings. It was very time-consuming, but productive and something I have not regretted.

It was now August 19, 2002, and the first day back to school for the girls. The school was only five minutes from our house. I was concerned because their education was going to be quite different here. Unlike the 200 students at their private school in California, their new school would have nearly 1,000 students. Their class size was nearly tripled. And I had no idea about the quality of the curriculum or the qualifications of the teachers. I had chosen the school not based on the education it offered, but rather on the fact that it was the largest Catholic school in Little Rock. I wanted the children to be immersed in the Catholic community in a state that was predominantly Baptist. Anything that was lacking in education I knew I could make up for at home.

Mom joined us that morning to lend a hand. As Halley and Madison got out of the car, I saw worried looks on their faces. They asked if I would come in with them. I said that my mom and I would walk them to their classroom. But after today, they'd have to be brave.

In their blue and white uniforms, we took each girl by the hand; Madison with me and Halley with Mom, while Anna Clare tagged behind. Inside there was a flurry of people shuffling about the halls. Children searched for their classes. Parents stopped to chat with one another.

I introduced Madison and myself to her teacher. She put her hand on Madison's shoulder and said how glad she was to have her in class. I could feel tears surfacing but smiled to prevent myself from crying and said to Madison, "How exciting that you are going to make new friends today. So when you get home, I want you to tell me the names of all the children you meet. I want to hear all about your first day."

I ran across the hall as Mom came out of Halley's room. I peeked in and saw her talking to another little girl. I went over to Halley, gently kissed her on the top of the head, and told her to have a great day.

When it was time to pick up the girls after school, Halley came streaming out of school into my arms, but Madison was nowhere to be found. I became worried immediately. *Did something happen to her?* I looked around in a panic. Nothing. Then I saw the principal coming out of the main entrance of the school, holding Madison by the hand. My little girl was sobbing. When our eyes met, she bolted straight toward me. I smiled and calmed her down. The principal explained that she got turned around and went to the wrong pick-up location. None of us had realized there were five different pick up points at the school. There had only been one at their old school.

After thanking the principal, we made our way to the car. Inside, Madison began to scold me. "Why did you send us to a school that was unsafe? Anyone could have grabbed me." She sounded just like her father; so reasonable and matter of fact about everything.

Later that day, the girls asked if they could go to a different school, a safer one, where no one could harm them. "There is a big fence that runs all the way around the school and the playground," I said. "Visitors have to check in at the office so the teachers know exactly who is in the school. It is very safe. But you have to know which door to walk out." We reviewed a couple of times where they were supposed to be picked up. After a few days, they felt more comfortable with their new environment. So did I.

Getting passed the first week of school allowed me to concentrate on how I was going to spend the first anniversary of Tom's death. I had several options. I had been invited to many memorial services, one in Reno, NV, one in Shanksville, PA, one in New York City, and several in California.

I decided to go to the memorial service in Shanksville. However, a few days after making that decision I realized I was not ready to take the girls to the crash site. Rather than spend the anniversary away from them, I cancelled my travel plans. That same afternoon, I received a phone call from the Frontiers of Freedom Foundation, based in Washington, D.C. They asked if I would keynote an event they were planning on September 10. I told them I would be glad to, but only if they could ensure my return home that same evening.

To share Tom's story in a political environment, with congressmen, senators, and businessmen present, would be a great opportunity. The event was also going to be covered by all the national broadcast networks. Because political leaders would be in the audience, this speech would be different. I wanted to address how important it was to use integrity in making decisions by sharing examples of how Tom lived his life. However, I also wanted to touch on immigration issues, the need for airline safety reform, and the need to expand the war on terrorism. Most of all, I wanted to plant the seeds of restoring prayer in our public schools as a tribute to those who died. My message and its reach were broadening.

The speech was well-received. Immediately afterwards, the people from the Frontiers of Freedom asked if they could post my speech on their website. I nodded. They further asked if I would consider being a contributing writer for their website and offered any help I may need in pursuing the issues I raised.

A cameraman from Fox News approached and quickly said, "I agree with everything you said. I'm not supposed to tell you that. But I wanted to anyway." I smiled and thanked him.

Then the president of the Young America Foundation introduced himself and asked if I would be interested in having them place me as a speaker at different universities around the country. Speaking and writing on a national scene sounded intriguing.

While in D.C., I had the honor of meeting the late Senator Paul Wellstone (D-Minnesota). He briefly talked about his meetings with the Burnett family and how much he enjoyed his time with them. I was impressed by his gracious demeanor and his eagerness to make a difference. As I was leaving, he asked if there was anything he could do for me. My first reaction was to say no. But then I said there was one thing. "I'd like the American flag flown in Tom's honor tomorrow over the Capitol." He immediately turned to his assistant and said, "Make it happen."

On September 11, the Burnetts and I launched a website for the Tom Burnett Family Foundation. Its mission is to educate youth to be active citizens and tomorrow's leaders. We wanted to memorialize Tom's strength of character by instilling values in children. I also thought that it would be a great way for my children to do good deeds in their father's memory. I knew it would be wonderful for Tom's parents and me to channel our grief in a positive way by giving back to a nation that had given us so much.

The foundation's goal was to have 50 college scholarships in Tom's name, one for each state. Over the course of a year, we hoped it would evolve into establishing leadership programs in the schools in conjunction with these scholarships. Tom often said that one of the noblest pursuits in life is to be a good citizen. We wanted these programs to help young people become more responsible and active in their community while developing leadership skills.

While I had planned to be home alone with the girls on September 11, 2002, my family insisted that I not be alone. They showed up at nine o'clock in the morning and kept me company throughout the day and well into the evening. At noon we attended a memorial service together at the cathedral downtown. The governor and mayor each spoke. Then I stood and I said a few words about Tom and his faith, drawing parallels between the differences in our lives today as opposed to September 11th one year ago.

I reminded the listeners that we had been a society of self-indulgence and unprecedented wealth. We debated morals and presented arguments as to what was right and wrong instead of recognizing there were absolute rights and wrongs. The traditional family was dissolving, and we had become a nation that had forgotten our obligation to teach our children by example and how to respect others. Then with the attacks on our country September 2001, our safety and security was compromised. The self-indulgent lives we had led seemed insignificant. We began searching for a deeper meaning to life. I wanted them to know that all of us could be heroes by living our lives as examples of honor, integrity, and courage. I wanted them to know it was important to have faith in God.

It was the first time my family heard me speak publicly. I glanced over at my family and saw each of them crying. I was continuing to do the right thing and their tears were a confirmation that my actions were having a positive impact. As time went on I would continue to look for new and broader avenues to bring forth Tom's message.

Deena Burnett with Anthony Giombetti

Fighting to Reclaim Lost Ground

"Victory is won, not in miles, but in inches." – Louis L'Amour

The first anniversary was over and it seemed everything halted. The phone stopped ringing. The mail was no longer overflowing. The media inquiries subsided. The outside world had gone away.

Anna Clare was in pre-school. Madison and Halley were in first grade. I regularly began to have time alone for more than half an hour in a row for the first time since Tom died. Finally, I was able to sit and really think about everything that occurred over the course of the year and let it sink in.

As I stopped to reflect, I found myself falling into a deep sadness. My energy level to do the things that needed to be done around the house dropped off. I was fighting depression again. I thought about a friend of mine whose husband had died several years earlier. I remembered encouraging her to get a pet. So I took my own advice and took in a stray cat. "Diamond" quickly provided great entertainment chasing birds around our backyard.

Like most mothers with houses bursting with infants and pre-schoolers, there had been a time in my life when I had dreamt of the days all three girls would be in school at the same time. I looked forward to using this time wisely and productively. I would also enjoy taking time for myself. In addition, for over a year I had craved normalcy in my life where there had been only chaos. Now the time had come. I could finally do some of the things I had been longing to do.

I realized that being a single parent meant needing to take better care of my health. I started exercising with Judy. We met each morning at the gym for an hour after dropping the kids off at school.

I started cooking again regularly and consistently. This allowed us to have dinner at home for a change.

I read some of the books Tom had suggested. *Fire in the Belly* by Sam Keen and *Undaunted Courage* by Stephen Ambrose.

I went to lunch with Judy more often and got to know her better.

I spent more time with my dad and grandmother, inviting them over at least once a week.

I was enjoying the down time and I was doing many things, but depression still lingered. I didn't feel like being social. When invitations came to different people's homes and for different events, I didn't feel like going. I had spent the last year simultaneously being pulled in so many different directions, surrounded by many people who wanted something from me. For now, I enjoyed being alone.

I cherished the quiet time and spent most of it reflecting and praying. I prayed that the decisions I made would be good, that I would be the kind of mother to my children that they needed, that we'd be able to make this a home and come to terms with our new life. And most of all I prayed God would make clear the direction He wanted me to go.

I already knew that if I didn't make an effort to get out and meet people and do things to become a part of the community, I wasn't going to be satisfied living here. So, again I made the choice to do the right thing. I would fight back. I would force myself to do the things I did not want to do. I would seek a balance. I would get out, but I would continue to make sure I had time alone as well so I could continue to heal and be refreshed.

The autumn days inched their way towards winter and Christmas. Since I had spent last year's holiday with my family, I decided we would spend Christmas with the Burnetts this year. Christmas Eve we celebrated at the home of Tom's sister, Martha. We attended mass at St. Edward's and then had a late dinner. A few of Tom's cousins stopped by for coffee and dessert. We exchanged gifts with those who dropped in. Someone came by dressed as Santa Claus. The girls were excited to see him. I was glad because I had neglected to get our annual photo with Santa at a mall this season.

Christmas morning with the girls was jubilant. They were thrilled to see so many gifts under the tree. The Burnetts had outdone themselves. Christmas lights sparkled. Mrs. Bev brought Mr. Tom and me a cup of coffee. Together we watched the kids rip through the packages. Tears welled periodically in Mr. Tom's eyes. Mrs. Burnett would turn away, then walk back and forth, pacing the floor. Occasionally, one of them would interject words of excitement, "Oh, look at that. You're so lucky."

There was clearly too much to unwrap. The girls had too many gifts and it was obvious I tried to make up for last year's somber holiday, too. The kids were becoming bored from opening all the packages and the overall mood in the living room was deteriorating quickly. Mr. Tom and Mrs. Bev were sad and I felt strange to be here without Tom on Christmas. It wasn't their fault, but I felt out of place. It was his family, not mine. There was nothing I could say to his parents to make everything okay. And I struggled with my own sadness that Tom wasn't here again to see his girls open gifts. I always felt when I was around the Burnetts I had to be strong for them. On Christmas it is hard to be strong, period. But it was all I could do to manage my own emotions.

We returned home on New Year's Eve. Because I didn't want my kids to grow up remembering sad holidays, I decided that from now on we would spend Christmas at home. We would visit the Burnetts after the holidays.

It was now 2003. We had passed the first year. I was better. We all were. But there was room for more improvement. I was tired of all the sadness in my life. I wanted people to know that I wasn't withering away. Yes, I missed my husband. Yes, I was sad my children didn't have a father. But I wasn't going to let this kill me. That was the choice. You either die or live through it. And I had been fighting all along to live through it. I wanted my heart to become happier so that smiling came naturally instead of always being forced. I didn't want to be sad anymore and I didn't want people to be sad for me. I wanted this year to be different. I knew I was the only one who could make it different.

As before I began concentrating on what I needed to do, on what I wanted to do to reclaim lost ground. I sought to be emotionally healthy and strong to make a difference in the lives of my children and in the world.

First, I signed on as a co-plaintiff in two criminal cases against Al-Qaeda members in Europe.

Next, if the house was to be a home, it was time for it to look like one. I began to consider how to furnish and decorate it.

I set financial goals for the Foundation and began planning a fundraiser to fill the coffers with the monies necessary to begin launching the scholarships and build the citizenship curriculum.

I volunteered to initiate and teach a Ministry of Mothers Sharing class at my church as a way of becoming more involved in the community.

And I accepted the offer to be a speaker for the Young America's Foundation.

In late February, I received a call from an attorney at Ron Motley's law firm, asking if would testify as a victim-impact witness against a member of Al-Qaeda. It would mean traveling to Hamburg, Germany for five days. He wanted me to know it could be very dangerous. I was given 24 hours to think about it.

The attorney made it clear that my going could make a difference in the outcome of the trial. He also explained I would have to leave the following week. Information regarding flights, hotels, and schedules would remain secret until I arrived at the Little Rock airport.

I didn't want to put myself and especially my children in danger. I was frightened, but I knew that participating in this trial was the right thing to do. If there was even a chance my testimony would make a difference in getting a conviction, how could I not participate? Because I didn't have much time to think about it, I called the priest at our church. I asked him to pray. I called my parents and explained the situation. They each discouraged me from going but would support any decision I made.

When the girls got home, I told them that one of the bad men who helped kill their father had been arrested. I explained to them that I was asked to testify in the trial. If I didn't go, then he may be released. If he was released, he may hurt someone else. They asked if they could go with me. I said no. They wouldn't be allowed in the courtroom. Halley and Anna Clare said I should go. They wanted me to make sure he was sentenced to spend his life in prison. Madison was afraid something bad might happen to me. She said enough people had died and to just leave him alone.

I spent the evening thinking about the conversations I had that day. I made copies of my will and testament. I made lists as to where all the legal papers were located and gathered bank account information. I even wrote letters to the girls. I put everything in the necessary order in the event I didn't come home.

A week later, four other family members of victims and I testified at the trial of Mounier el Motassadeq. The courtroom was nothing like I had ever seen before. I was taken aback by a wall of bulletproof glass which separated the galley from the witnesses, defendants, and judges. It was a constant and gut-wrenching reminder of how serious the trial was.

In my address to the court, I testified about my husband, who he was, how he lived, and what he did on September 11th. I told them how as a result of the terrorist's actions my children would have to grow up without a father. I showed the court photographs even though I was told not to. I wanted the court to see that the lives of real people had been devastated and changed forever by the attacks.

Holding up pictures of my daughters, I told the court how they write letters to their dad and stuff them into helium-filled balloons, hoping that angels will carry their messages to him in heaven.

"My request to you," I told the court, "is to demonstrate the same courage displayed on Flight 93, by holding the defendant responsible for his criminal acts of terrorism and murder. I hope that like my family and me, you too will be inspired by Tom's words, to do something."

After the trial, on the plane home, the man in the seat next to me began to chat. When the flight attendant handed out newspapers, he realized who I was. The trial had been covered by every newspaper around the globe. My photograph was in the one he was reading.

He began to speak of his own difficulties. He had lost a lot of money in the stock market. His wife had run up the credit card bills. He had taken a pay cut at work. He was forced to trade in his car for a lesser model. And he wasn't sure how he was going to make his house payment. He also was concerned about not being able to put money in his children's college fund. After learning who I was, he said he felt guilty being depressed over something as unimportant as money when I had suffered the loss of my husband. Turning to me he asked, "How do you do it?"

I wasn't sure how to respond. His situation was very different from mine yet he seemed to be grieving in a similar way. I looked at him and simply said, "Be grateful for what you have instead of consumed by what you have lost."

Tears filled his eyes and he grasped my hand. I hoped that I had been able to help. Fighting back, standing for what was right, whether in things the world considered big or small, it didn't matter. Both were important. Each represented doing something. They each made a difference.

It was spring and this year it represented not only a rebirth of the land, but also a rebirth of our household. I felt better. I had more energy. I reveled in the blooming flowers – the azaleas, daffodils, dogwoods – and found myself looking forward to the heat of the summer. I was coming alive. I was beginning to feel things again instead of existing in numbness. It felt as if a veil had been lifted. It felt good.

It made me want to fill the empty rooms in our house with laughter and people. Back in California, I had always enjoyed having the girls' playmates over, my friends for brunch, and big dinner parties. I wanted that again. I was ready.

We had been in Arkansas almost a year, and I hadn't invited anyone over because there was no place to sit. I'd been too preoccupied to shop. One evening I met a friend of Judy's who owned a furniture store. She offered to help. The next day she came over and looked at the house. Two days later she returned with three large trucks filled with furniture. I was blown away.

As I watched, the drivers placed furniture in one room after another. If I liked how everything looked, it stayed. If the furniture didn't look right, they put it right back on the truck and something else would come in. She gave me a precious gift. Furnishing my home, which had become such an obstacle for me, she resolved in one day. By the time she left, there were pictures on the walls, accessories on each table, and a rug on every floor. The house was beautiful.

Next on my mind was a fundraiser for the Foundation. I decided on a golf tournament. Tom had loved golf. The San Francisco Bay Area was a logical venue because people knew and supported us there. They would want to be part of the work being done in Tom's honor.

My friends and neighbors from San Ramon were willing to help. They pulled together and organized everything from promotions to the event itself. The girls and I showed up in August 2003 for the tournament. It was an incredible event that raised over $100,000 for the Foundation. Now we had the money to begin placing the "Citizenship Education Curriculum" in schools around the country.

Tom's niece, Kathleen West, an 8th grade teacher in Minnesota, started the program in her school. Her efforts served as a great prototype. The curriculum teaches students to be proactive members of their community. It encourages responsibility, builds leadership skills, and promotes community service. It encourages students to find purpose and see value in serving others beyond themselves. The students benefit by realizing the impact they can have on the world around them. Concurrently, as the students begin to do the right thing, it also builds their self-esteem. The program culminates on Tom's birthday, May 29, when the participants perform a community service project that they plan and organize.

The second anniversary of Tom's death came and went. Young America's foundation scheduled my first speaking engagement. It was at Harding University, not far from my house. I continued speaking wherever opportunities presented themselves, from church groups to civic organizations. The size of the venue didn't necessarily matter, the objective was simply to get the message out.

The content of my speeches began to change. I always told Tom's story, and I always talked about my faith. But the message evolved from challenging people to be good citizens to talking about how all of us can be heroes.

Expanding on the issues I first mentioned at the Frontiers of Freedom event over a year ago, I used the platform I had given through Tom's death to express my thoughts and ideas. Speaking on college campuses gave me an opportunity that churches did not. I was able to address a broader group of issues, such as the war on terror, abortion, prayer in schools, profiling, and voting. All the while I was coming to terms with how different my life was and fighting back daily to make sure the future was painted with a silver lining.

Five years have now passed since September 11, 2001. I continued to make choices to fight back for what I believe is right in my personal life and on the world stage.

I had decided early on to make sure our children understood who their father was, what he did and why. But Tom worked so much there were also many things he had wanted to do, but hadn't. While Tom had goals of high achievements, he also had dreams of simple things. In keeping with Tom's memory and the plans he and I made for the girls, I now made a conscious effort to do the things he wanted to do, but his schedule would not allow.

We learned to snow ski and fully enjoy our ski trips each year. We fulfilled the dream of our family having a horse. My dad fenced in his

3-acre pasture, providing space and care for a 14-year-old mare, Toby. The girls ride western style. We go out every Sunday afternoon, weather permitting.

Tom had insisted I learn how to play golf before we married. After I had children, I rarely had the time. Once Anna Clare started school, I began taking golf lessons with a friend. I enjoy the challenge and the quiet time the game allows.

Tom always laughed at my lack of gardening skills. I have always loved flowers, but I would never stop to take care of them. Now, I not only take the time to *"stop and smell the flowers,"* I also grow them.

Even though Tom was of the younger generation, he was often treated as the patriarch of his family. His opinion was sought and his decisions were not questioned. As his wife, I saw Tom as the intermediary between his parents and me. After his death, the dynamic of the Burnett family changed where my relationship shifted beyond that of a passive daughter-in-law. Though we were no longer related, we were bound by the tie of my children and the circumstances surrounding Tom's death. Oddly enough, by developing a mutual respect for one another, his parents and I have become friends.

Our work in establishing the Tom Burnett Family Foundation allows Tom's memory and his actions to live in perpetuity. Having a curriculum that teaches children a value system and leadership skills will provide, for generations to come, a stronger America.

The lawsuits against United Airlines and the terrorist networks, while ongoing, have already provided a wealth of information. The United suit has ruled out some of the questions concerning the actions of the security company and whether there was a jumpseat rider in the cockpit. The Saudi suit has assisted our government in the War on terror by providing information as to the identity and whereabouts of terrorists. We have been told that this information has been beyond legally helpful. It has literally saved the lives of many of our soldiers. Even if there is never a resolution in court, the suit has been a valuable tool in fighting for truth and preserving what is good.

The outcome of the Al-Qaeda trials in Germany was not what we had hoped. Motassadeq was sentenced to the maximum of 15 years. He appealed and was re-tried a year later and convicted on lesser charges. He would serve a maximum sentence of seven years. Abdelghani Mzoudi, who was charged for an alleged role in the 9/11 plot, was acquitted of the charges due to the lack of cooperation on behalf of the U.S. Government in providing witness testimony from Binalshibh, an Al Qaeda member in U.S. custody. I was sorely disappointed, but have never regretted trying to do the right thing by testifying.

I still do a lot of public speaking. My topics continue to evolve from encouraging the audience *to do what is right* to challenging them to consider *what are you willing to fight for.* My willingness to speak to a variety of groups has given me the opportunity to become politically active in a way I could never have imagined. Through being aware of the impact one person can have, I volunteered for the 2004 Bush-Cheney campaign. I soon found myself speaking at various political events, including the 2004 Republican National Convention.

Tom and I both realized the importance of our political leaders having strong character. I have thought so many times about how ironic it is that George W. Bush came into his own as President on the day my husband died. My work on his campaign was not only rewarding, but I saw it as a very personal tribute to my husband.

I was also a guest speaker at a "Support the Troops Rally" in Crawford, Texas in 2006 to encourage our country to understand that the war we are fighting on terror is necessary to ensure our future freedom, just as the actions by the brave passengers of Flight 93 were. If we are to preserve what we have, we must fight back.

Regardless of the subject or the venue, whenever I speak my goal is to always bring glory to God and honor to Tom and our family.

I've been approached with the idea of running for a political office...House of Representatives and Lieutenant Governor. While both are intriguing, my children are my priority. It would be too difficult to raise them the way I intend if I were bound to an office of serving the people. It remains in the back of my mind, and perhaps will come to fruition when the girls are grown. In the meantime, I am happy to continue speaking and being an active American citizen.

At the encouragement (or shove) of a few very good friends, I began dating again. I am currently engaged and by the time this book goes to press, I will be remarried. I don't have to wonder whether Tom would be happy for me. I know that he would. He once told me that not only would he want me to remarry, but he would expect me to. He believed in the importance of a two-parent household and wanted his children to have a father as well as a mother. I've met a lovely man with a heart big enough for all of us as well as for the life of active citizenship I will continue to lead. The girls have come to love him, too. I think somehow, he is heaven-sent.

Deena Burnett with Anthony Giombetti

Conclusion

"Do not be overcome by evil, but overcome evil with good."
– The Bible, Romans 12:21 NIV

Tom made his choice. I continue to make mine. Doing the right thing, is usually not the easy thing to do.

For me that has meant stepping out of the quiet suburban life in which I took such pleasure. Then speaking out to remind the world of the values which give life its foundation and purpose. With teeth gritted and a stomach nauseous from stage fright, I accepted the public platform in which Tom's last choice put me. I am using it to share Tom's message with you now. I believe this is the right thing.

Tom fought to maintain freedom in order to preserve our country and the values upon which it was founded for our children and our children's children. I choose to continue that fight. We are all called on in our own way to be good citizens, to do the right thing with an objective for the greater good, which looks beyond ourselves. We are called to stand up, press on, do the right thing and when necessary, fight back.

Sometimes our weapons against that which threatens our values will be our fists and a meal cart like on Flight 93. Sometimes it will be our kindness that overcomes malice, our gentleness that overcomes anger, or our mercy and forgiveness that overcome self-condemnation. There will be times when doing the right thing will mean giving a hug or providing a meal. There will be times when we must stand firm, stand up and speak up, fighting against that which seeks to destroy what we stand for by working through governmental channels and persevering until change has come to pass.

Each situation in which we find ourselves everyday may require a different tool, a different weapon to do the right thing. We must be alert to what our circumstances require. We must be vigilant, diligent, and persevering; humble enough to admit when we are wrong and continually strive to learn more. We must listen to our hearts which can hold wisdom from God which exceeds human logic.

For several decades our country has been heading in a moral direction which is wrong. Yet we have been unwilling to admit we are off-course and have justified our actions by muddying the boundaries. However, what is right remains right. The clear difference between right and wrong is founded on eternal principles established by a supernatural God and not humanity. Those who are willing to do what is right need to stand up. It's time to fight back.

– THE END –

Deena Burnett is available for speaking engagements and personal appearances. A portion of the proceeds will benefit the Tom Burnett Family Foundation. For more information, please contact:

TOM BURNETT

FAMILY FOUNDATION

"DO SOMETHING"

Deena Burnett
Tom Burnett Family Foundation
PO Box 26014
Little Rock, AR 72221
Phone: 501-868-5811

To order additional copies of this book or to see a complete list of all **ADVANTAGE BOOKS™** visit our online bookstore at:

www.advbookstore.com

or call our toll free order number at: 1-888-383-3110

*A*dvantage
BOOKS

Longwood, Florida, USA

"we bring dreams to life"™
www.advbooks.com

Printed in the United States
58312LVS00004B/61-63

9 781597 550376